A TIME

TO MEND

A Time

To Mend

Reflections in uncertain times

Peter Millar

wild goose
publications

www.**ionabooks**.com

Overseas distribution
Australia: Willow Connection Pty Ltd, Unit 4A, 3–9 Kenneth Road,
Manly Vale, NSW 2093
New Zealand: Pleroma, Higginson Street, Otane 4170, Central Hawkes Bay
Canada: Bayard Distribution, 10 Lower Spadina Ave., Suite 400, Toronto,
Ontario M5V 2Z

Printed by Bell & Bain, Thornliebank, Glasgow

Contents

'… and a time to mend …'

– Ecclesiastes 3:7

*For Dr Runa Mackay
who has done so much
to make this world
a better place*

Foreword

Over sixty years ago, George MacLeod, Presbyterian churchman, Celtic mystic and founder of the Iona Community, wrote:

What I find in the Bible ... is precisely that God is to be found in the material. *And that He came to redeem us, body and soul. The Gospel claims the key to all material issues is to be found in the mystery that Christ came in a body, and healed bodies and fed bodies, and that he died in a body, and rose in a body: to save us body and soul.* (From a sermon, 1948)

This profound truth – that a human being is a unity, body and soul, and that God is intimately concerned with, and ultimately to be found within, all matter and all life – has been for me, as for millions, a reality that I have had to grow into, sometimes painfully, at times even reluctantly, but increasingly with gratitude and joy. It's not a truth that is always honoured within the Church – and certainly in our northern, Western world, where it's more often than not dismissed as an embarrassment, with its central meaning frequently rejected in favour of rampant individualism, consumerism and cynicism.

Peter Millar has made it his life's work not only to try to live out this truth, but to witness to it in his writings, some of the most powerful of which are gathered here. A Church of Scotland minister and world traveller, he has made it his business to go and live alongside the oppressed, the dispossessed and the marginalised in India, South Africa, Australia, South East Asia and many other places. There he has lived not as an outside observer, never as one bearing gifts, but always as a companion in the fullest sense of the world: as someone coming, quietly and humbly yet with a deep desire to learn, to 'share bread' with his hosts. And then, where he could, to speak truth to power, without favour and without fear, in a world now increasingly to be known as one world.

In these writings, you will find compassion and anger. You will find, not optimism, but hope. You will find wisdom and prophecy, poetry and prayers. You will find, time and again, Peter's firm conviction that, as he puts it, *'our common heartbeat connects us all'* – that, *'when all the chips are down the divine power of love is embedded in the human fabric in such a way that the accumulated ills and wrongs of the centuries are never the final word'.*

Many centuries ago, Saint Augustine from North Africa wrote: *Hope has two daughters. Their names are Anger and Courage. Anger at the way things are, and Courage to change them.*

Peter has embodied this insight over many years. He has suffered for it – and struggled with it. It is by God's grace that we are given the opportunity to journey with him, in these and his other writings. It is surely to be hoped that there will be many more to come.

John Harvey

Introduction

About three years ago a friend said to me that he enjoyed my books but thought I should write something more regularly about the connection between the Christian faith and what is going on in the world.

So began my monthly reflections, which now go out to many parts of the globe. I try to keep them short and to the point! Many of those who read these reflections send me comments and responses and I greatly value all of these. An interesting e-mail and letter dialogue has developed with many people, some of whom are living in situations of great hardship. I also like the fact that many who send me messages are not believers in any traditional sense, but are still searching for spiritual meaning in their lives.

Neil Paynter, who is as many know an indefatigable editor at Wild Goose Publications, suggested Wild Goose bring out a book which would include some of these reflections – and this is it! Of course you don't need to agree with my views, but if they start you thinking in fresh ways about faith in God in these uncertain times, that will be great. I try to write from a tender heart, and like many others I experience days of desolation and questioning. Through it all I continue to believe in God, but I understand why many are unable to share such a belief.

I have called the book *A Time to Mend* because I recognise that we do need many signs of healing in the world. Much is breaking down, and in many countries the extent of human suffering is almost unimaginable. But surely if our age is marked by such uncertainty and disconnection then compassion, awareness, hope and risk-taking for truth are needed more than ever. I know that millions of us believe that. And what inspires me is that in every situation of human suffering there are 'the menders'. Those who don't give in to greed or violence, but who walk the extra mile for others. These women and men are in fact holding us together, and regularly in my monthly reflections I try to celebrate their life-affirming journeys.

A Time to Mend. Or to put it another way: a time to affirm again *'God's goodness at the heart of humanity. A goodness planted more deeply than all that is wrong.'*

Peter Millar

A gift without price

Pray together

With the whole church
WE AFFIRM
THAT WE ARE MADE IN GOD'S IMAGE,
BEFRIENDED BY CHRIST, EMPOWERED BY THE SPIRIT.

With people everywhere
WE AFFIRM
GOD'S GOODNESS AT THE HEART OF HUMANITY,
PLANTED MORE DEEPLY THAN ALL THAT IS WRONG.

With all creation
WE CELEBRATE
THE MIRACLE AND WONDER OF LIFE;
THE UNFOLDING PURPOSES OF GOD,
FOREVER AT WORK IN OURSELVES AND THE WORLD.

– Affirmation from the morning service in Iona Abbey

In a world of many tears
we search each day
for markers of hope:
for the small unexpected signs
of light and love;
for the quiet assurance
that goodness is planted
more deeply
than all that is wrong

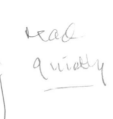

read quietly

and that one day
the captives will go free.

And sometimes on the journey
we discover a gift without price:
the balm of understanding
deep within our soul.

The knowledge that, despite everything,
'we are companions of God
in the work of creation':

wounded healers
even when weeping ourselves;
bearers of justice
even when overwhelmed;
witnesses of hope
even when struggling to survive.

For Light still shines,
and illumining our days
we walk together in it.
And in the walking
we remember and celebrate
the miracle and wonder of life –
but also something more:
the unfolding and surprising purposes of God
forever at work in ourselves
and the world.

The pilgrim path

Experiences of
Iona ?
other pilgvenin, togetherness
— solitude

Christians can be described as 'the pilgrim people of God', and in the Bible this idea of the spiritual life as a journey is expressed many times. Through the centuries, pilgrims have come to places like Iona seeking healing, inspiration and redirection.

The outward pilgrimage is a sign of this inner journey – of repentance, resurrection and rebirth – the journey of the heart, held in the Creator's hands. It is rooted in the conviction that life itself is a process of continual change and movement. We are never static, and we carry within us a sense of expectancy, of looking forward in hope.

The writing to the Hebrews framed that reality in some memorable words: '*Therefore, since we are surrounded by so great a cloud of witnesses, let us also lay aside every weight and sin that clings so closely, and let us run with perseverance the race that is set before us, looking to Jesus the pioneer and perfector of our faith*' (Heb 12:1, NRSV). Here is expressed that marvellous journey of the Christian soul, on a continuing pilgrimage into the heart of God – a pilgrimage which will never be completed here on earth, but continues in God's wider Kingdom.

Places like the island of Iona are, in a particular way, associated with pilgrimage, but the pilgrim path is located everywhere and never just in sacred places. The question remains: are we open to being a pilgrim? Are we prepared to live with some of the risks and uncertainties and loose ends which pilgrimage always entails? The pilgrim can never have everything neatly 'sewn up' – there is always the exploration, the search, the movement, the questions and the challenge.

Prayer

Challenging God,
may we who are pilgrims
follow you
into the hard places
of peacemaking,
of embracing the earth,
of making our voice heard in the marketplace,
of refusing to tame your gospel
in a world of easy compromise.

Ireland

Guguletu journal 1:
terrible suffering, but also resurrection

Some years back, when Kathy Galloway was Leader of the Iona Community, she received an invitation from the Revd Dr Spiwo Xapile, minister of a large Presbyterian church in the township of Guguletu near Cape Town. The church has an ongoing support programme for those with AIDS, and Spiwo asked the Community if they could send a member for some weeks to help the congregation reflect theologically on this important ministry and to walk alongside some of those people.

The Community sent me. As my journals make clear, to be living in the township was a privilege and my neighbours there taught me much about the things that really matter in our journey here on earth. I hope some of their love and courage comes through in my writing ...

This morning I was in the principal's office in one of the local schools here in the township, and this was on the wall in English (not Xhosa, which is the main language in Guguletu). It was in large, bold print. I thought at first it was a Bible text, as they are popular in local schools:

THE LORD LOOKED UPON MY WORK
AND WAS VERY PLEASED.
THEN HE LOOKED AGAIN AND SAW MY SALARY.
HE TURNED AWAY AND BOWED HIS HEAD ... AND WEPT.

I turned to the small group of teachers who were in the room. 'Yes, the Lord is certainly weeping,' one said.

And that same Lord also must be weeping over the lack of basic school equipment, over parents who cannot afford to give even one decent meal each day to their kids, over the five young mums who were buried in the local cemetery last Saturday, over the division between rich and poor in this beautiful land, over the guy who said to me this afternoon, *'I am HIV-positive and I'm living with a tsunami inside me.'*

Sure there is much weeping here … but also hope.

Phumzile Mabizela, who is one of the team here at the J.L. Zwane Memorial Church in Guguletu, and who herself is HIV-positive, reminded me one day, as we were working together, that, amidst the suffering, we need *'theologies of life'.* When Phumzile said that, I thought of an insight of Rowan Williams. In a reflection on the Beatitudes written for the Christian Socialist Movement, Rowan wrote: *'We need not only have moralism or despair. There may be such a thing as vitalising anxiety – an ache about the transformation which keeps us alive, which keeps us sensitive.'*

Perhaps what has struck me most is that alongside the sorrow in Guguletu there is this *'vitalising anxiety'* which allows suffering people to retain not only their hope but also a deep concern for their neighbour. And these twin realities of hope and concern are powerfully reflected in the Sunday worship here. And this ability to live with a certain optimism of spirit is lived out in a context that most of us cannot imagine. As if years of oppression under apartheid were not enough, no sooner had the bells of freedom rung out across this beautiful land, than HIV/AIDS descended, especially upon the poorer families. As one South African doctor put it: *'This country is fast proceeding up the AIDS sickness and death curve.'*

The late Cardinal Basil Hume said that in the face of vast human suffering there are two authentic responses in the human heart: the first is compassion, and the second is silence. Basil Hume, a man of deep prayer, was right. Silence and compassion taken together can be transformative. In what ways they are transformative cannot be easily defined. Yet yesterday afternoon in a tiny but tidy room as I gently stroked the incredibly thin, bruised arm of a young bedridden mum gasping for breath and almost unconscious, I knew that she was comforted. In her agony, she was not alone. In fact we were both held in God's tender embrace. That was what mattered. And it was real. To some it may sound strange or crazy, but in that place there was both dying and healing. Terrible suffering, but also resurrection.

Guguletu journal 2: the struggle for daily bread

'Even if I am a poorest person, it is important to keep everything clean.'
– Words of a young mum in the township

'Six of my family have died of AIDS. There must be a reason.'
– Words of one of the women who work alongside HIV/AIDS folk

'If you can't preach or sing, just dance.'
– Words of a member of the church, at a home prayer meeting before a burial in Guguletu

It is a special experience to stand at the open window of my room in Guguletu at about 9 o'clock in the evening. Across the vast, surrounding township, dim lights twinkle beneath a clear Southern sky. Sometimes there is singing, sometimes laughter, sometimes shouting, often loud music. But it can also be quiet and still, as most families are afraid to be in the streets after dark. And then into that wide, comforting canopy of stars come the evening flights from Jo'burg and Durban, and close behind them a succession of international flights, reminding us that the humble homes here in Guguletu are part of our profoundly contradictory global connecting.

Cape Town's airport is very close to Guguletu, but most of the community here – although they can watch dozens of flights a day – never board these planes – nor are they ever likely to. For the families here don't have the remotest possibility of two weeks in Florida, or even a short holiday in their own beautiful land. The struggle for daily bread and shelter does not give birth to many options for living. A reality for the majority of humankind.

Yet last Sunday at the morning service, Spiwo Xapile, the minister here whose enormous vision has done so much to help uplift the local community, spoke strongly about the work ethic. He was reflecting on a passage in John 21 in which the disciples caught nothing in their nets; so Jesus told them to cast them on the other side of the boat. In other words, to look at an alternative way of doing things.

Spiwo has been working in Guguletu since 1988, and is convinced that even the poorest of the poor can find within themselves new resolve, and not always expect others to help them. He used a wonderful example in his sermon, which brought much laughter in church. He said we pray to our dead ancestors to win the lottery even though they themselves never won it. In other words, we look for solutions outside ourselves, whereas we must struggle to stand on our own feet.

Spiwo also reminded the large congregation – made up of folk of all ages – that during the years of apartheid, black South Africans saw work as linked to exploitation, which it was, and so did as little as possible, in order to make the country unworkable. Now that attitude must be turned around. Blacks, he said, speaking as a leader in the black community who has come from a humble home in a rural part of the Eastern Cape, must be prepared to work as hard as possible in the new South Africa.

Given the enormously high unemployment rate in the townships, the church itself has initiated many job creation schemes, so is very much walking the walk as well as talking the talk.

Guguletu journal 3: theologies of life

Lord, bless the journeys we never planned to take,
but through your surprising wisdom
discovered we were on.

It is a few years since I wrote this prayer, and in the intervening time there have been many surprises in my life. One of the purposes in my coming to Guguletu was to engage in theological reflection with the community here around the whole issue of HIV/AIDS. To be honest, I don't think I have contributed much to the local theological awareness in Guguletu. It is already profound and vibrantly creative. On the other hand, the folk here, and especially those who survive against all the odds, have taught me so much. I would say that they invite me to look at an engaged Christian faith through a new lens, and not just because their lives are filled with a range of struggles. They are also a people who walk and sing with an integrated spiritual knowledge often missing from my own life.

The AIDS pandemic compels us to face the reality of human suffering. My experience here is, in a sense, superficial: I am not living in a shack that leaks (there have been very heavy rains recently), with another seven people in the house, one of whom – a young dad with three children – is lying desperately ill with full-blown AIDS, nursed by his wife who is herself HIV-positive, and all of them wondering where the next meal will be coming from. (No, I am not trying to paint a worst-case scenario, but simply describing a family situation in a home near the church.)

Given the pressures that many families are facing daily just to survive in Guguletu, it is, in one sense, almost abusive to reflect theologically as a visitor, despite the warmth of the welcome I have received. As I think of my own life, I accept that it is earthed in a group of securities, many of which are unattainable here – my good health, a balanced diet and a comfortable pillow on which to put my head at night in a home that does not get sodden when it rains. Yet my head on its soft pillow has many questions. In what way is my comfortable life linked to the tears of Guguletu? Am I just imagining that I can be in solidarity with the families here? What does it mean to say that the caring, often desperately poor families here are my sisters and brothers?

It has struck me again and again how inadequate many of our 'theologies of suffering' are – most of which have been constructed far from the narrow streets of Guguletu. While as I visit the homes here and sit alongside local people, one of God's rich surprises is that I am more often than not encountering *theologies of life*. It is these theologies of life, grounded in human suffering, which are today prophetic not only for South Africa but for the world church. They are channels of transformation.

A few days ago, I visited a home where the mum had died of AIDS. It was a home filled with sorrow, yet as we shared the bread and wine and remembered a strong and courageous woman whose glorious singing had filled this home, God was in our midst. As some of the church members began to sing a familiar Xhosa hymn, I felt that humble home becoming a 'thin place' where the spiritual and material worlds were interwoven. There was no separation, nor could there be, for God understood the cries of our hearts.

Guguletu journal 4: Noma-lady's prayer

'I think I've at least six things going against me these days: I'm poor; I'm unemployed; I'm HIV-positive; I've had my legs amputated; I'm black and I'm gay.'

— A member of one of the local HIV/AIDS support groups in Guguletu

'People are often shocked by the things I talk about during the workshops. But until I was trained as an AIDS educator I myself would not have used words like "condom". I tell people that they should know more about sex and AIDS than I do because I'm a Catholic nun, and yet I am the one who has to teach them these things.'

— Sister Immaculate of the Franciscan Nardini Sisters

'I love them with all my heart.'

— A single woman who is fostering seven orphans in her small home

'I used to attend the local church but I don't any more. The pastor there believes that you can't be a Christian and have HIV. Two of my friends from the church used to keep telling me not to take any medicines, just to trust in Jesus to heal me. I couldn't accept that. I want to have Jesus and keep taking medicines. So I don't go to church any more, but I pray every morning for my family, for my son, for the doctors and for everyone living with HIV/AIDS.'

— Maria, a 30-year-old mum

Here at the church in Guguletu, where I am based, the ministry with those affected by HIV/AIDS is inspirational. There are many dimensions to it. Each day of the week, many people, all of whom are HIV-positive, receive a cooked meal, as a decent diet is so important and difficult to obtain. There are numerous support groups and counselling groups and a team of home-carers who visit throughout the community. At the Sunday morning service each week there is a time when a person who is HIV-positive shares their story. Noma-lady, who is a local woman with AIDS, shared a beautiful prayer in her own language, Xhosa. A friend has translated it. It is a prayer which has touched me deeply and made me aware of the powerful way in which those faced with suffering speak to us all:

God is love to me – and God is amazing even though I am not strong physically in terms of my health. Even though things are difficult, I continue to go down on my knees and pray, and from time to time I see God responding to my prayer. I don't know how.

I don't know how I could praise God's name in a way that is befitting God's greatness.

I do not have the instruments appropriate enough to make the music that would truly express how I feel about God. There are times when I have sleepless nights and watch TV till morning, but I always feel comfort when I go on my knees and pray. I am sometimes up at 3am trying to sleep on that side or the other. There are times when the pain is so heavy, my hand with cramps, my fingers twisting. Had I not been connected with God I would be accusing people of causing this pain, but earlier in my life I chose a close relationship with God, though I am poor. God is with me in the morning when I wake up, God is around during sleep, and is with me as I try to walk around. I just cry knowing that God has heard my prayer. I live with great hope. Amen

Guguletu journal 5: Phumzile's letter

In Guguletu I have many special colleagues. One of them is Phumzile, and this letter which she sent me brought me closer to the experiences of a black South African woman, whose heart of compassion reaches out to many:

Dear Peter,

Every step of the way I truly believe God is preparing me and moulding me for the special role I am supported to play within our changing reality in a free South Africa. A freedom for which my brother, at 26, was murdered by the secret police. We will face many struggles to make this country a place where all can walk with dignity and equality.

I was born 40 years ago in a township in KwaZulu-Natal. Both my parents were factory workers. We always had good, but my parents hardly ever had time with us. I had to grow up very fast and take my mother's role as she was at work most of the time. Spiritually we had a unique balance between our African traditional and Christian beliefs.

The African rituals which my parents respected and faithfully observed were totally separate from and unrelated to the 'church God'. There may have been some similarities, but the prayers and language used were totally different. For the 'church God' there were prescribed prayers. Prayers to ancestors were about real issues like expressions of gratitude for well-being and requests for solutions to family problems. There was a sense of closeness and importance during these rituals. However, the unwritten code was that the 'church God' was superior and had more power and authority. As a young person this caused confusion. I started to rebel. The more I tried to make sense of my faith, the more confused I was.

Most people in our neighbourhood were not desperately poor, although life was hard in many ways. Most of the parents at that time had jobs in factories which were 8 kms from our township. Poverty only started showing its ugly head when people started losing their jobs and the rates of unemployment increased.

All the issues that affect people in my country, and more specifically the community I work with here in Guguletu, form an important part of my ministry. As a black HIV-positive woman, the issue of gender inequality and its effect on the increase of HIV and AIDS infection is priority. I have used my own story and struggles to encourage others to claim their place within the Kingdom of God. We also openly challenge anyone who thinks they have a right to undermine or discriminate against us.

I have two boys and a daughter. Mnqobi is 20, Manqoba, 15 and Sthandiwe is 3. I was a single mother for a long time. I was married to Sbongiseni in 2001, exactly three years after being diagnosed as HIV-positive. God is good – my daughter is HIV-negative and I am not sickly. The community in Guguletu is very supportive, and I am now much involved with the ministry to those who are HIV-positive. My husband is not with us here in Guguletu because he has a job in KwaZulu-Natal, which is more than 1000 kms away. We believe that as time permits he will move to Guguletu. The freedom to follow my dreams and be in a job which I enjoy is an advantage that most African women do not enjoy. That is why a huge part of my job is dedicated to empowering women to realise the importance of claiming personhood, created in the image of God, and providing them with space and tools to read and interpret the Bible in their own liberating way.

When I was diagnosed as HIV-positive I thought my world was ending. I knew God was with me, but did not know how to relate to God. I think 'praying' was replaced with deep heart-to-heart talks with God. I had to choose between life and being controlled by the virus. I chose life, which was the beginning of a new life for me. With God's help my priorities have changed and I choose my battles carefully. I read the Bible as a black woman who is HIV-positive. This approach has made me strong each day. When I hear judgemental and discriminatory interpretations of the Bible, I sympathise with the interpreter. They usually speak out of ignorance. Whenever there are opportunities to challenge these interpretations I do so with a lot of love.

The God I talk to is more like a woman and understands my language. My joys and struggles. I can openly express my feelings with and to God, even feelings of anger. I love the woman I am becoming. The God I try to serve is bringing out the best in me!

My greatest hope is that one day we will all be recognised as gems created by God, irrespective of our pasts, gender, race and economic status. I believe that by undermining and despising those who are not like us, we miss out on important lessons and gifts. God is revealed to us through unconditional acceptance. I suppose this is a huge order! But I believe that we should strive for it.

I think I can truly say that I am beginning to appreciate, love and sing about the different aspects and facets of God. I still have a long way to go! Through all our struggles we know we can be strong – and lovely.

Your friend,

Phumzile

Guguletu journal 6: it cannot shatter hope

It was on a warm May evening that I left Guguletu for the long journey home to Scotland. The township is only a few miles from the airport but I was accompanied on the ride by Xolani, a fantastic footballer in a local team who had become a good friend. Guguletu's often crowded streets were quiet as we headed to the N2 motorway which skirts many of the vast townships of the Cape Flats. I would soon be in a very different world and one into which very few from Guguletu ever enter: the often bizarre world of international travel.

I said my farewells to Xolani, and a couple of hours later the twinkling lights of Guguletu were far below. But I was still there in my heart and in my thinking: with Linda Goba who 17 years earlier had been caught in crossfire at her front door and who has been paralysed ever since; with Noma-lady, so weak with AIDS, whose incredibly beautiful prayer had touched my heart; and with Bandile, a young man whose caring work reaches so many in the community. And I also thought of some words given to me a few days earlier by a local person critically ill with AIDS:

AIDS is so limited.
It cannot cripple love.
It cannot shatter hope.
It cannot corrode faith.
It cannot take away peace.
It cannot kill friendship.
It cannot silence courage.
It cannot invade the soul.
It cannot reduce eternal life.

It cannot quench the spirit.
Our greatest enemy is not disease
but despair.

It has been such a privilege to share in the lives of many in the township. These last weeks in Guguletu have also raised many questions in my mind. Questions about God, about the nature of human suffering, about death and dying, about global economic structures, about the increasing divisions between rich and poor in South Africa and elsewhere, about oppression, about the struggles for justice, about the courage of the soul, about 'theologies of life' in the midst of pain, about the role of the churches in South Africa, about our domesticated Christianity in the UK, about the importance of sharing our stories, and about prayer and healing.

And I would like to end with some words from *Witness to AIDS* by Edwin Cameron, a judge of The High Court in South Africa, who himself has AIDS. Nelson Mandela describes Edwin as one of South Africa's new heroes. In this book he addresses the taboo questions of race, sexual orientation, poverty and stigma in the context of the HIV/AIDS pandemic, writing from a personal perspective, but with an unconditional commitment to social justice. It is also an invitation to all of us to thread our compassion with *hope*:

We cannot escape our grief or the losses we have experienced or the suffering that has been ... we cannot allow our grief and our bereavement to inflict further loss upon us: the loss of our own full humanity, our capacity to feel and respond and support. We must incorporate our grief into our everyday living, by turning it into energy for living ... (From *Witness to AIDS*)

33

Lord of the morning

Lord of the morning,
I awake to
this new day
with all its possibilities,
its uncertainties,
its risks,
and its underlying mystery.

May I be able,
in your strength,
to move through this day
free of inner anger
or outward irritation,
so that when
I meet my neighbour
or encounter a stranger,
I may recognise
your face.

Global protest at predatory capitalism

During the long years of struggle against apartheid in South Africa, the local churches there brought out a powerful statement which they entitled 'An Affirmation of Faith'. These words have a contemporary relevance at a time when many people in the Western world are protesting about the injustices surrounding what is termed 'predatory capitalism' (as opposed to productive capitalism).

The South African document contains these words: *'It is not true that our dreams for the liberation of humankind, our dreams of justice, of human dignity, of peace, are not meant for this earth and this history.'* In other words: God's justice is to be felt in our midst, in the here and now. Not only in heaven, but also on earth.

Around the world people of all ages and of all faiths are saying that enough is enough in relation to our present-day pervasive predatory capitalism. We see this protest expressed in the Occupy London and Occupy Wall Street campaigns. These protests are opening up a long-needed debate about unbridled capitalism and about the ethical bankruptcy which lies at the heart of many global financial institutions. This moral vacuum within financial structures has become clearer to the general public following the bailout by governments of major banks. It is also reflected in the growing divide between rich and poor. As the German theologian Hans Küng said: *'Society does not need a uniform religion or a uniform ideology, but it does need some binding norms, values, ideals and goals.'*

Today, when we read some church pronouncements, we could be tempted to think that human sexuality was the number one moral issue in the Bible. Years ago, George MacLeod, the founder of the Iona Community, spoke about the unbridled power of financial institutions as being a central moral issue when we take the Bible seriously. He wrote prophetically about the *power of the money boys* in modern societies. His insights were spot-on. Predatory capitalism is out of control. But not only that, in subtle and less subtle ways, it controls us all. And moral evil in high places is still moral evil, however much it may be clothed in power, status and a knowledge of market forces.

There is a growing awareness and a legitimate anger about the unjust ways in which wealth is distributed. But there is more at stake. Many of those who believe in such protests also know that society needs a paradigm shift. As one protester put it: *'We want to change minds and hearts.'* To raise fresh questions in all our minds: Why cannot real change take place? Why are these institutions not more accountable for their behaviour? Is it inevitable that the gulf between rich and poor becomes wider year by year? The British journalist Madeleine Bunting described the aims of the protest in this way: *'It is about seeding questions in thousands of minds, shaking certainties and orthodoxies so that there is space for new alternatives'* (*The Guardian* 30/10/2011).

And while the protest against this rampant capitalism may be secular, the issues which it raises about wealth are both theological and spiritual. Pope Benedict has demanded that capitalism and the financial markets be brought under a *'world authority'*. Yet it is not only the Pope who sees that something is sick at the heart of the markets. People of all faiths share a profound moral revulsion at the almost unbelievable gulf

New Pope Francis 2013!

between those earning millions, who still demand more, and the millions existing on less than a dollar a day. At the heart of contemporary capitalism are dark shadows which must be brought to the light of day. For those who try to follow the path of Christ, this issue illumines what is demanded of us when we say that 'God is justice'. A truth summed up by the prophet Isaiah: *'I, the Lord, have called you and given you power to see that justice is done on earth'* (Is 42:6, GNB).

There is also another important dimension within the protest movement. The protesters in London chose the steps of St Paul's Cathedral on which to camp out. St Paul's is one of the grandest churches in the country and it stands in the heart of London's financial district. Wren's great building is surrounded by some of the world's leading financial institutions, and within a short distance from its High Altar millions of pounds are traded every hour of the working day. Perhaps hundreds of millions.

Giles Fraser, who was at the time of the protest a canon at St Paul's, shared the convictions of the protesters, who remained on the Cathedral steps for several weeks. He talked for hours each day with those who were there and valued the range of their ages, nationalities and the complex and interesting mixture of views which they held. Yet he also saw how united they were in their legitimate anger about the way in which wealth is distributed. He was also impressed by the sense of mutual caring which was a characteristic of the protest, and by the thousands who came from near and far to support the campers living in tents erected on the church steps.

In an article which he wrote during the protest, Giles said, *'The interesting thing about the protest camp for me is that St Paul's is very, very good at doing the grandeur and otherness of God. You can do fantastic sermons in it about creation, mystery, otherness, grandeur. But Christopher Wren's forte was not Jesus born in a stable, the sort of church that exists for the poor and for the marginalised'* (*The Guardian* 27/10/2011).

In Edinburgh, where I live, we had a much smaller group of protesters, but it was a privilege to share in discussions with these concerned people. Many of those who were camped out in one of Edinburgh's main city-centre squares were people who had reflected deeply on the injustices which flow from the present global money structures. Like me they were concerned about our human future, which so easily could become inhuman. They knew there are no easy fixes. The road to greater justice and accountability is both long and hard. Yet what allows hope to flourish is the fact that many people across the world want to be on that road, and to give time and wisdom to bringing about a change in our consciousness. A new way of seeing how money works.

Scott's sermon of 22/9/13. —The parable of the rich man's servant.!

An alternative narrative

In this time of predatory capitalism it is important that people of faith keep reminding society of an alternative narrative. And that narrative – expressed in all the great religious traditions of the world – reminds us of certain basic elements needed to retain our humanity.

For several years, my late wife Dorothy and I, along with our three children, lived alongside many poor families in South India. That was a privilege. These Indian families taught us so much about what it means to be a rich human being. In terms of money and possessions they had little or often nothing at all, but in terms of the human spirit their wealth was limitless. Even the poorest family would make sure we had food before we left them. Sharing what they had was not something to be analysed. It was a fact of daily living.

The present belief in grabbing all that we can for ourselves raises many questions. Is it possible in our modern technological societies to reconnect with a culture of giving, of sharing? To ask seriously of society and of one another: what actually are our rights, responsibilities and privileges? Is it possible, as the old saying puts it, *to learn to live more simply so that others may simply live?*

These are political questions, but they are also questions for people of faith. Even within our secular societies many still believe in God, and with the understanding that we are in a fundamental way accountable to each other, and that we are stewards of the sacred earth in all of its diversity, beauty and wonder.

It is also true that our daily living can reflect an alternative narrative. Through our elected representatives and other channels thousands are campaigning against the culture of greed. That is a great hope in such times. We can all do something to express another way of living. We have choices, and – despite its many flaws – most of us who read this are living in a democracy. Our voices can be raised in the public square without fear of persecution.

Gandhi's words are not new, but they are relevant in the struggle to witness for truth and for a renewed understanding of how human beings should interact with one another (and not only in his native India where recently millions have taken to the streets to fight against the rampant corruption at every level of Indian society):

'To recognise evil and not to oppose it is to surrender your humanity; to recognise evil and to oppose it with the weapons of the evil-doer is to enter into your humanity; to recognise evil and to oppose it with the weapons of God is to enter into your divinity.'

Wisdom from India

One day
when living in the great city of Chennai
in South India,
I opened *The Indian Express*
and read these words by a local person,
Mr N.K. Somani:

'Let us teach our children one lesson:
the act of dispossession.
Life is an opportunity to evolve,
not to indulge.'

Guru Nanak and truthful living

When I read about the conflicts between the different religions in modern India, a country which was my home for several years, I think back to the vision of people like the Sikh scholar Guru Nanak (1469-1539).

Indian philosophers and saints of the 15th and 16th centuries belonged to an age of spiritual development where the concern was not only with the inner mind, but also with a person's whole being and activity. Faith and daily actions could not be separated, and we saw this truth being expressed in the way great souls like Gandhi and his colleague Vinoba Bhave led the movement for the independence of India in the last century.

The work of Guru Nanak, and of the subsequent Sikh Khalsa movement, was astonishingly original and renewing. It was an outburst of fresh creativity, based on an assimilation of the past, but looking to the future. Guru Nanak saw that the great religions of India must live in harmony, each tradition respecting the rituals and belief systems of the others. He said: *'Truth is high, but higher still is truthful living.'*

Our media in the West show the violence rooted in India's religious conflicts, but it is also important that we honour the communal harmony which is present in many places. In every part of India there are ordinary people giving their lives for what Guru Nanak called *'truthful living'*. And, like Gandhi, they continue to inspire our human family.

From the 17th century comes this Sikh prayer, by Govind Singh:

> *Lord, Thou bestowest love and Thou givest thyself to all;*
> *Thou art the protector of life and the giver of blessing;*
> *Thou art the cure of all sorrow and suffering.*
> *In all shapes and everywhere, Thou art dear to me.*
> *Thou art our vow, our beginning and our end.*

Journey of the soul

inner confusion
inner light,
inner flight
inner grounding,
inner angst
inner song,
inner voices
inner growth:

inner tears
inner joy,
inner chaos
inner wisdom,
inner struggle
inner quiet,
inner voices
inner growth:

inner storm
inner peace,
inner delusion
inner calm,
inner grief

inner hope,
inner doubt
inner faith,
inner voices
inner growth:

inner healing
inner silence,
the soul alive –

thankful
that the day is
blessed
and the journey goes on.

Accepting difference

In 2009, in Malawi, the gay couple Tiwonge Chimbalanga and Steven Monjeza were sentenced to 14 years in jail with hard labour: because they loved each other.

There was international condemnation of this judgement. The British government, Malawi's biggest donor, expressed dismay, but did not withdraw aid or apply any sanctions. The US State Department said it was a 'step backwards in the protection of human rights'. Michelle Kagari, deputy Africa director of Amnesty International, called the sentence 'an outrage'. She said that Amnesty would 'work tirelessly to see that they are released as soon as possible'. On 29 May 2010, the then President of Malawi, Bingu wa Mutharika, pardoned both individuals. In May 2012, President Joyce Banda announced his intention to repeal the law criminalising same-sex sexual activity.

Some years ago, in my book *Waymarks: Signposts to Discovering God's Presence in the World* (Canterbury Press), I wrote:

Thankfully, but often slowly, we are awakening to the acceptance of 'difference', which includes, among other things, our sexual orientation. For some, this is an incredibly tough learning process; for others a vibrant expression of maturity within our human journeying.

I have found that it sometimes feels like being at the foot of a great mountain when I suggest that in accepting a person's sexuality — genuinely accepting it, as opposed to agreeing to a vague idea that people are different — we are acting normally! That we are not going mad, or acting strangely or going against the will of God.

As I read the Gospels, I am always struck by the fact that Jesus met people where they were in life. It may sound trite, but he saw their potential and valued their essential humanity, often in circumstances where other people only regarded them as walking disasters. And it is in this valuing of the human person that we can move into new depths of understanding, insight and awareness about one another, whatever our differences.

A prayer which is used in Iona Abbey includes the words, 'Lord, your image deep within us.' The image of God imprinted in the human person: every individual carrying those sparks of divinity which are markers of our Creator's energy and wisdom.

The journalist Andrew Sullivan, writing about his own experiences as a gay man in *Virtually Normal*, reminded his readers of our interconnected humanity, whatever our sexual orientation may be. With many others I feel sad that gay, lesbian, bisexual and transgendered people throughout the world still have to keep reminding others that they are first and foremost human beings. Made in the divine image, as we all are.

The following words, which I wrote some time back, reflect my own long and often painful journey in learning to value both my own sexuality and the sexuality of others. Throughout that journey, my late soul mate Dorothy was always a companion and a light, and I often think back to her profound understanding of accepting difference in others. Dorothy was always able to see the creative potential in other people and to walk with them on their own road. To celebrate who they were, and to know that we all carry vulnerabilities, strengths and multiple contradictions. All of us – without exception!

As I come to a mellow, even peaceful awareness
of my limited grasp of truth,
I don't need to defend myself
against people or experiences
which might hold new or challenging information.

I become open to these truths
that reside
half-hidden,
and often surprisingly,
in my own and others' journeys.

And this is a gift,
a rare treasure –
freeing me to understand
rather than to be understood;
calling me

to fewer words,
to awareness,
to humility,
to patience,
to laughter,
to tenderness,
to listening,
to waiting on that God
who always
welcomes home
a mellow heart.

Created in love

God, let's celebrate –
for you never see us as
Muslim or straight,
poor or Sikh,
gay or rich,
Christian or black,
but as persons created in love
and bearing your image.

On war and peace

Everything that happens in this world happens at the time God chooses. He sets ... the time for killing and the time for healing ... the time for war and the time for peace.

– Ecclesiastes 3:1–8, GNB

You are going to hear the noise of battles close by and news of battles far away ... Countries will fight each other, kingdoms will attack one another.

– Matthew 24:6–7, GNB

'*We cannot go back to operating as we might have done even 10 years ago when it was still tanks, fast jets and fleet escorts that dominated the doctrine of our three services. The lexicon of today is non-kinetic effects teams, counter-IED [improvised explosive devices], information dominance, counter-piracy and cyber attack and defence ... Attacks are likely to be delivered semi-anonymously through cyberspace or the use of guerrillas and Hezbollah-style proxies.*'

– General Sir David Richards of the Ministry of Defence in the UK, speaking in September 2009

A couple of years back, thanks to the kind invitation of my elder son Eldon, I was at Buckingham Palace in London. On that day, Eldon was being honoured by his country for his outstanding and courageous leadership in the war in Afghanistan. I was proud of Eldon, as any dad would be on such an occasion.

As he went forward to receive his honour, I was thinking not only of

Eldon but of his many colleagues who have been killed or seriously wounded in Afghanistan. I am sure he was also thinking of them because his pastoral care and concern for the women and men under his command has been a central component of his leadership. Not only in Afghanistan, but also in Iraq, Bosnia and Kosovo.

But on that summer morning in London, surrounded by the pomp of the British monarchy, I was also thinking of the many local women, children and men in countless towns and villages in Afghanistan who have been victims of improvised explosive devices. Their names and narratives are largely unknown to us, and we shall never know in detail the terrible daily sufferings they too have endured because of war. War in their own land.

And millions of us around the world continue to ask what is the purpose of this war in Afghanistan which is taking many lives and birthing so much sorrow. When will it end? How will it end? How many more will die? Are people on both sides dying in vain? What is the future for Afghanistan? And what of the war's cost? Endless questions. And these questions, along with countless others, are being asked in many countries and across the board. Not only by folk in the streets, but also by our politicians and by military commanders. I hope that they are also being asked by the Churches, for this is a theological, moral and spiritual issue for all Christians.

It is not easy to work and campaign for peace and justice in the modern world. We all know that. The global military machine is far beyond the understanding of individuals, and words such as those from General Sir David Richards, himself a good and honourable man, send a chill down our spines. Yet without our military in place, would the world resort to total anarchy? And what of the role of the military as peacekeepers within a world of multiple conflicts, both large and small?

Centuries ago, those who wrote the Bible seemed to accept, as they reflected on God's purposes and the human condition, that war and conflict were inevitable. They accepted that there were times of war and times of peace. Times of breaking down and times for building up. In the New Testament, Jesus and his disciples announced the possibility that one day our world may become conflict-free. I will not see such a day in my lifetime. Yet the invitation to look at our human condition through the eyes of non-violence, of creative love, is always present, as Gandhi in the 20th century so powerfully reminded us.

It is my conviction, as it is of many others, that we must continue to speak of the possibility of peace in our world. Ordinary women, children and men in every country on earth long to live their days in some degree of peace, even if that word 'peace' means many different things. But there are also those who do not seek peace, and sometimes we find that a hard truth. The addiction to power often leads to conflict, and that striving for individual power is also at the heart of human experience.

Through my elder son's work as a respected military commander and strategist, I have come to a range of new understandings about our world. Over these last several years that has not always been an easy journey for me, and I value the support of friends and colleagues in it, and their untiring support for Eldon, especially when he is working in areas of high danger.

51

But surely the truth is that we are all on a journey of understanding when it comes to the complex issues of war and peace. Yet it gives us all hope that the Bible writers were themselves on a similar path. They accepted the reality of conflict while at the same time illumining for us a pathway to a more tender acceptance of each other. I tried to express this biblical wisdom in a prayer:

> *God, illumine our minds as never before.*
> *Let us forgive this century and every other.*
> *Stop the war in ourselves and in the world.*
> *Remove from our hearts the illusion that we are separate.*
> *May every nation and every culture*
> *recognise the pain of our common fears*
> *and discover that one amazing heartbeat*
> *we all share.*

The single heartbeat

Across our world
upon the just and unjust they fall –
these markers of our age:
missiles from on high,
birthed in technology at a cost of millions.

And only when we hear the cries of pain
and make them our own,
will we meet the One who,
in holding all our tears,
draws us into a single heartbeat.

For against all the odds,
and often in dark times,
that connecting of souls still propels
our uncertain human journeying
as it ceaselessly and silently moves
within the immensities of space.

A letter to Lorna and John Norgrove

In October 2010, Dr Linda Norgrove, an environmental scientist from the isle of Lewis off the west coast of Scotland, was taken hostage by the Taliban in the eastern province of Kunar in Afghanistan. Linda had been working in Afghanistan with the charity Development Alternatives, helping local farmers. She was greatly loved by both her colleagues and the local people, whose language she spoke. Linda was killed as American Special Forces tried to rescue her. Several of those who had been involved in her kidnap were also killed in this complex rescue mission. Her parents, Lorna and John Norgrove, live in Uig on Lewis, and Linda is buried close to the family croft there.

Dear Lorna and John,

Although I do not know you personally, in these last weeks I have been walking with you in your sorrow following Linda's death. I know that many around the world are also walking with you and with your loved ones at this time. I know that everyone on Lewis shares in your grief.

It is just wonderful that you have recently established the Linda Norgrove Foundation which will be able to help many families in Afghanistan. I am sure there will be a terrific response to your initiative as there are many compassionate people everywhere.

I have felt particularly identified with you at this time, as my elder son, Eldon, who is the same age as Linda, has also been deeply involved in Afghanistan, although in a different way. Last year, Eldon was a military commander in Afghanistan and was recently honoured for this work by our country. Several of his colleagues were killed, and many others seriously wounded. Like Linda, Eldon is a person of compassion and awareness. A deeply insightful human being in this divided world. He also believes in the search for peace, just as Linda did.

For many years my late wife Dorothy and I worked alongside marginalised communities in South India. Our three children were brought up there. We shared Linda's valuing of cultures and traditions different from our own. Part of our own work in India was also involved in development, and sadly some of our colleagues there were killed because they spoke out for lasting justice for those on the margins. When I heard of Linda's death I wept for her – and for those other friends who had given their lives in order to bring more justice to others. Truly, Linda will continue to be an inspiration for all of us who long for a more just world. It is not surprising that many both here and in Afghanistan mourn her passing.

I also understand something of your personal sorrow. Dorothy, my soul mate, who had given her life and energies to make this a better planet, died some years ago, in an instant, from a massive blood clot. She too was mourned by many around the world, and part of her compassionate vision is remembered through the work of the Dorothy Millar Trust.

Even though I miss Dorothy hugely, I know that many good things have resulted from her sudden death, and I am sure this will be true following Linda's death. It seems paradoxical, but Linda's tragic death will have galvanised people in many different places to discover new dimensions of compassion and of understanding. It will also have brought home to thousands of people some of the realities of daily life in Afghanistan. The realities which face ordinary children, women and men every day.

In my own life I try, rather falteringly, to follow Christ's teaching, but I respect and greatly admire humanist views and know from the many tributes to her that Linda was motivated in her work by a profound love of and respect for human beings. That is what matters. Our common heartbeat connects us all. It is tragic that today at least some of the world's violence and hatred is due to religious dogmatism of one kind or another.

I admire the way in which you both have spoken about the need not to apportion blame for Linda's death, and such a stance is inspirational at a time when many public figures and others rush to place blame on others. Thank you for responding to your own personal tragedy with such grace and insight.

In 1998 our home was on the island of Iona, and in December of that year, four of our young people from the island were drowned together on a December night in the Sound of Iona. The island came together in grief. It was very special. I am sure the same is happening for your family on Lewis. And those who mourn with you on Lewis are joined by many around the world. And that in itself is a sign of hope in our divided world. Human connection.

Thinking of you – with sympathy and warm wishes,

Peter

www.lindanorgrovefoundation.org

Celebrating sanity

Are the longings of our hearts
so strange, so misguided,
so out of touch with our times?

We who companion the forgotten;
who seek the healing of nations;
who cry for justice:
who struggle for peace,
who envision a different world.
Are we mad to speak of hope
as thousands die in flames of violence?

Be still, my friend, and celebrate your sanity!
Keep to that path where the Spirit befriends us,
for millions walk with us and share our dreams.

Sounds of the forest

Creator of all,
we often forget
that you are alive
in the leaping salmon,
in the sounds of the forest,
in the gentle rain,
and in that tender stillness
of a long summer evening
when your world seems at peace.

So help us to pause,
to remember,
and to smile
as we think of the beauty of it all.

An Australian apology

It's Wednesday, 13th February, 2008. A warm wet morning in Sydney, where I am at present. This day will go down in Australian history. A few hours ago, the new Labour Prime Minister, the Mandarin-speaking academic and former diplomat Kevin Rudd, said 'Sorry' on behalf of the nation for the pain, suffering and hurt experienced, over generations, by indigenous Australians. *The Sydney Morning Herald* put it this way:

> *With just 361 words, the Federal Parliament will today seek to heal the hurt caused by past decades of state-sponsored ill-treatment of all indigenous Australians – not just those forcibly removed as children from their families.*

> *More than 10 years since the story of the Stolen Generations* was told in the* Bringing Them Home *report, the declaration of the apology will usher in a new era of recognition and reconciliation between indigenous and non-indigenous Australia …*

> *The apology will follow yesterday's official opening of the 42nd Parliament, which for the first time included the local Aboriginal people, who performed a 'welcome to country' ceremony.*

> *Mr Rudd and the Opposition Leader, Brendan Nelson, vowed that the ceremony would be a permanent feature of future parliamentary openings.*

These are the words of the nation's apology:

Today we honour the Indigenous peoples of this land, the oldest continuing cultures in human history.

We reflect on their past mistreatment.

We reflect in particular on the mistreatment of those who were Stolen Generations – this blemished chapter in our nation's history.

The time has now come for the nation to turn a new page in Australia's history by righting the wrongs of the past and so moving forward with confidence to the future.

We apologise for the laws and policies of successive Parliaments and governments that have inflicted profound grief, suffering and loss on these our fellow Australians.

We apologise especially for the removal of Aboriginal and Torres Strait Islander children from their families, their communities and their country.

For the pain, suffering and hurt of these Stolen Generations, their descendants and for their families left behind, we say sorry.

To the mothers and fathers, the brothers and the sisters, for the breaking up of families and communities, we say sorry.

And for the indignity and degradation thus inflicted on a proud people and a proud culture, we say sorry.

We the Parliament of Australia respectively request that this apology be received in the spirit in which it is offered as part of the healing of the nation.

For the future we take heart; resolving that this new page in the history of our great continent can now be written.

We today take this first step by acknowledging the past and laying claim to a future that embraces all Australians.

A future where this Parliament resolves that the injustices of the past must never, never happen again.

A future where we harness the determination of all Australians, Indigenous and non-Indigenous, to close the gap that lies between us in life expectancy, educational opportunity and economic possibility.

A future where we embrace the possibility of new solutions to enduring problems where old approaches have failed.

A future based on mutual respect, mutual resolve and mutual responsibility.

A future where all Australians, whatever their origins, are truly partners, with equal opportunities and with an equal stake in shaping the next chapter in the history of this great country, Australia.

A few hours after the apology was announced many of us gathered together for an ecumenical service of prayer and thanksgiving. During the service one of the participants shared this beautiful prayer which touched all our hearts:

Loving God, we place before you the pain and anguish of dispossession of land, language, lore, culture and family kinship that Aboriginal and Torres Strait Islanders have experienced. We live in faith that all people will rise from the depths of despair and hopelessness and experience your healing Spirit.

* In Australia, the term 'Stolen Generations' refers to the many thousands of indigenous children who, in the first 70 years of the 20th century, were forcibly removed from their families and communities through government policy.

The hovering spirit

A letter from Australia to friends in Scotland ...

Dear Sally and John,

At present I am in the Northern Territory of Australia living alongside indigenous people. A place of the hovering spirit! Travelling under the bright evening stars in the stillness of this desert outback is to be in touch with something of that mystery which has been understood by Aboriginal people for over forty thousand years. Yes, forty thousand – and many scholars think a lot more than that!

Your own existence feels so temporary in this vast landscape, formed over tens of millions of years. Yet I also feel deeply at peace: held in nature's beauty and in its silent invitation. This extraordinary landscape reveals its truth through desert skies, flame-red rocks, ancient pathways and hidden springs filled with sweet water. It has a cosmology all of its own.

Throughout the millennia, Aboriginal people have developed an understanding of this cosmology: the natural forces of the earth, the inhabitant flora and fauna, indeed the total cosmos in which man, woman, animals and natural phenomena are linked. And today this vast canvas of knowledge, which was essential for human survival through the centuries, continues to be evoked in song, poetry, ceremony and amazingly beautiful ritual painting. In fact I have just returned from spending a couple of hours with an Aboriginal elder who is also a fine painter.

As I try to take in these dimensions of knowledge I become more and more convinced that the survival of the human race is dependent on us recovering at least some awareness of their sacred interconnectedness with all that lives. It's not possible to do that in the same way as Australia's indigenous people, and it would be wrong to try to do so, yet in beginning to accept that we inhabit a sacred universe (and not one that can be constantly dominated by human greed) we awake to these paths of interdependence and interconnection.

Aboriginal spirituality is so grounded and practical. The Australian author David Tacey wrote a book about emerging spiritualities within his own country: *Re-enchantment*. In this book, David makes a strong plea for an earthed spirituality, and in reference to Aboriginal knowledge of the sacred says this:

> *For Aboriginal people, the 'natural' way to live involves also a supernatural, mythological or imaginal dimension, and yet this supernatural dimension is eminently realistic, since it commands respect for the land, restrains human brutality and urges us to relate to the environment with love, reverence and awe.*

I think this is immensely helpful as we seek to discover a spirituality of connection with the natural order. In Christian thought we are sometimes starved of imaginal dimensions in our attempts to connect theology and the good earth. Yet we need not be. It is hugely exciting that we can listen to cultures such as that of the Aboriginal people and in a certain sense be transformed by them, even if our understanding is limited. And if that sounds like a contradiction, then it is!

I am grateful for this experience of living in a remote community. The warm winds of the hovering spirit are around and this vast silent land lying beneath a cloudless sky has at its heart many songs.

Shalom,
Peter

Old man banksia*

God of bush and bog myrtle,
of old man banksia and dancing birch,
of sheltering banyan and red rowan,
of whispering aspen and huon pine,
of heather and eucalypt:

illumine our minds
that we may embrace
your sacred earth
with a renewed tenderness
imbued with wisdom
and rooted in wonder.

* Banksia is an Australian wildflower.

65

Reawakening to mystery: a journey home

Apprehend God in all things,
for God is in all things.

Every single creature is full of God
and is a book about God.

Every creature is a word of God.

If I spent enough time with the tiniest creature –
even a caterpillar –
I would never have to prepare a sermon.
So full of God is every creature.

– Meister Eckhart

Grandfather Great Spirit,
all over the world the faces of living ones are alike.
With tenderness they have come up out of the ground.
Look upon your children that they may face the winds
and walk the good road to the Day of Quiet.

Grandfather Great Spirit,
fill us with the Light.
Give us the strength to understand,
and the eyes to see.
Teach us to walk the soft earth as relatives to all that lives.

– Sioux prayer

A sense of mystery is central to a meaningful life, and not an escape from it – a source of healing threading through the everyday.

Yet how do we recover this consciousness of mystery when we have grown up in a culture which is essentially hostile to anything which cannot be proved by science?

One of the facts of life on the island of Iona is that each day one comes face to face with the elements – rain, wind, sunshine, thunderstorms and rainbows. It was the same for Columba and his monks over fourteen hundred years ago, and in a thousand, or fifty thousand, years from now, these elemental forces will still sweep across the remote beaches and gentle hills of that Hebridean isle. It is not surprising that many regard Iona as 'a thin place', where the material and spiritual dimensions of life are separated only by a veil, *as thin as tissue paper*.

But for most of us, our lives are in the thick of the city, within concrete and steel landscapes far from sea-girt islands. We do not see space as 'sacred' and are often violently disconnected from the natural order and from that pervasive sense of intimacy with it which characterised the lives of our forebears. Amidst the mind-blowing achievements and certainties of technology it is not difficult to lose our sense of mystery.

The writers of the Old Testament lived with the knowledge that humanity had always been faced with the divine mystery. From the very beginning, human beings had been in the presence of mystery. Hebrew religion springs from this encounter with and exploration of the sacred mystery.

In Hebrew the word for sacred mystery is *elohim*, a plural form which originally must have meant 'the gods'. It was a word signifying the whole world of the gods, that is, the sacred mystery itself. With the coming of Abraham, the founder of the people of Israel, came the experience of a transcendent God who manifested himself in the history of a particular people. But it was through the symbols of mystery, such as flaming fire, that Abraham received God's revelation. It was the same with the prophets: God revealed through water, cloud, fire and thunder.

For a thousand generations, human beings viewed themselves as part of this wider community of nature, and they carried on active relationships not only with other people, but with animals, plants and the natural world, including mountains, rivers, winds and weather patterns. Human beings knew that they belonged and were 'at home' in this wider frame of meaning, as is so evident from the prayers of my own Celtic forebears.

For many of us today, this journey into the rediscovery of mystery is essentially a 'journey home' into our fuller identity as God's people. It is not a running away from the realities of the contemporary world; nor is it some elitist concern. I believe it is the opposite. It is a coming to terms with the basic fact that our lives must be earthed in the humble acceptance that we travel on this earth lightly and provisionally; that we have no permanent resting place; that God holds out to us grace-filled moments when we simply stand in awe and are silent at the wonder of it all.

Reawakening to mystery; returning home and finding ourselves at one with God's vast and interdependent universe; seeking the humility, grace and tenderness that comes from being fully a part of that incredibly diverse sacred whole, a truth illustrated in some lyrical words by David Abram:

An alder leaf, loosened by wind, is drifting out with the tide. As it drifts, it bumps into the slender leg of a great blue heron staring intently through the rippled surface, then drifts on. The heron raises one leg out of the water and replaces it, a single step. As I watch I, too, am drawn into the spread of silence. Slowly, a bank of cloud approaches, slipping its bulged and billowing texture over the earth, folding the heron and the alder trees and my gazing body into the depths of a vast breathing being, enfolding us all within a common flesh, a common story now bursting with rain. (From *The Spell of the Sensuous*)

Accepting mystery

Why can't we accept that
life is
mystery
despite the vastness
of our knowledge?

'Unfathomable'
is the word
that comes to mind
in relation to ourselves
and the world.

Some disagree, and say
that all of life
is understood,
codified,
apprehended.

But stand beside me
on a wooded path
on a glorious
early-summer morning
as tender mist
lifts silently
from Highland hills
while overhead
an eagle soars,
and tell me then
that all can be explained.

Returning home

Returning to God is a lifelong journey.

– Henri Nouwen

As a deer longs for a stream of cool water, so I long for God.

– Psalm 42:1

Returning home, in the sense of discovering that God walks with us on our journey, takes a lifetime. Wisdom is not going to come in one minute! Yet so long as we are willing to take risks, be open, work for justice, love the earth, reach out to our neighbour, and travel within, we shall discern many waymarks – often some truly amazing ones.

Kenneth Leech, who is both an Anglican priest and a prophet for our times, speaks of *'the energy derived from yearning'*. I think that is a wonderful phrase – affirming, challenging – and one from which all seekers can find inspiration. It is God's energy that lies within our yearning. It is part of our human condition to have restless hearts – but it is these often contradictory journeys of the soul which connect us to the One who created us. It is not possible to have a static spirit. The Danish writer Soren Kierkegaard put that truth succinctly when he wrote that *'we are always* becoming *people of faith'*. In other words, life is a pilgrimage: a movement into God who pervades the whole of creation.

And our search for God's wisdom takes place amidst the ordinary experiences of life: within our fragmented lives which run in several directions at the same time. I believe that profoundly, which is why this poem finds its roots in the fluctuations and bewilderments of my own existence. They are the words of a 'seeker after truth' who believes in a God who never answers all our questions, but understands far more clearly than we do where they come from.

Am I alone in yearning for
the recovery of vision,
of authentic outrage,
of gentle connectedness,
of the truth that sets us free?

Do you tell me that such idealism is impossible
in a world of
junk mail,
easy money,
fleeting icons,
fragile relationships
and grinding poverty?

With you I ask,
can the miracle of God's light
permeate
all this?

Can we still hear
that single voice of Love
through these myriad cries,
or see in our neighbour
the face of God?

Can the angels
stop us in our tracks
as we relentlessly
seek life elsewhere?

My friend,
in our shared uncertainty
we stand with our peoples,
broken like them;
but also –
propelled still
to befriend
the amazing and unpredictable
wisdom of God.

In a low beautiful voice: from Bethlehem

	1948	1998
Jewish population of Israel	600,000	4,850,000
Palestinian population of Israel	250,000	950,000
Palestinian refugees	700,000	4,200,000

– Statistics posted up at a guest house in Jerusalem

Every authority in Israel, beginning with the state of Israel, its institutions and employees, must treat the various individuals in the state equally.

– Aharon Barak, former Chief Justice of the Supreme Court of the State of Israel

I'm afraid the coming generation is being pushed into a place where there seems to be no room for coexistence any more.

– From a Palestinian NGO network

It was a glorious sunny November morning in Jerusalem. Around lunchtime my friend Colin and I boarded the 124 bus for Bethlehem. It was full, and after 10 minutes we all had to get off as we had reached the checkpoint into the Palestinian territories. How can one describe the solid, concrete, 630-kilometre separation wall (farcically called a 'fence') – in some places 25 feet high, and built at a cost of billions of US dollars – which now encloses much of Palestine? To enter the actual checkpoint is to walk into a concentration camp. Our passports were checked twice, and after that, along with many local folk, we walked through a long, narrow alleyway which is enclosed on either side by 15-foot-high steel fences. On exiting this abominable fenced-in walkway we boarded another bus, which carried us to Bethlehem. But many others have to walk the few miles into town, often bearing heavy loads.

As many of us know, Palestinians are made to stand for hours at these checkpoints, often in blazing sunshine, on their way to and from work – that is if they are fortunate enough to have work, for unemployment is at a staggering level. It's hell – a daily hell – experienced by tens of thousands of all ages, and often involving abusive treatment from the security guards, who are young Jewish women and men. Dr Martin Luther King was right when he said: *'Our lives begin to end on the day we become silent about things that matter.'* Why are the nations silent when faced with such evil? And the short answer, as we know, is vested interests: land, money, power, prestige, religion, oil – an endless list. The wall that now straddles this wounded land and imprisons so many is also a reminder of the dark side in us all. I – with many others – am complicit in this hell, this oppression of a nation, and Christ weeps not only over modern Jerusalem but also over my silence in the face of such wrong.

In central Bethlehem the Church of the Nativity was packed with pilgrims from many countries, a beautiful and powerful reminder of the extraordinary diversity of the world church. For a few moments we joined a group of Africans in prayer – that vibrant kind of praise and thankfulness to God which resides in the African soul, and knows what it means to have faith in hard times. And I thought again how true it is that often those in the shadows are the ones who reveal the true nature of the divine. In a place like this, in a town under oppression, the words of Mary carry a deeper resonance and fresh questions for our wounded world: *'The Lord has brought down the powerful from their thrones and lifted up the lowly; he has filled the hungry with good things and sent the*

75

rich away empty' (Luke 1:52–53).

As we walked across Manger Square, Colin suggested that we visit the mosque, which for many generations has stood directly opposite the Church of the Nativity. Many worshippers were going in and out, but no tourists. We asked if we could enter and were given a warm welcome. As we ascended a wide staircase to the central prayer hall, a Palestinian man in his 60s asked where we came from. We started to talk and he told us that he was one of the two muezzins at the mosque. He had been calling the faithful to prayer five times a day in this particular place for 31 years; we soon recognised that we were in the presence of a holy person. After introducing us to the imam, he led us up a narrow, stone spiral staircase to a small balcony which tops the minaret. The view across the villages, valleys and hills of Palestine was literally breathtaking. And on the far horizon, the wall – which looks ghastly at any time, but much worse beneath the brilliant sun – snaked its way amidst the fields and olive groves, dividing communities and families in its relentless progression. Below us the bells of many churches rang out, while on the far side of the square an Armenian bishop got into the back of a small rather decrepit taxi, while in the front seat a young priest held an enormous gold cross – which stuck out of the window by at least five feet. No hiding of the faith here!

And then a very special thing happened: our newfound friend said he would like to sing for us. In a low beautiful voice he sang from the prayers which have companioned his life on earth these last 31 years in the mosque. It was an unforgettable moment. He then translated his songs for us, and as we shared together, he said, *'How can there be peace in my land if our hearts are angry and not pure – whether it be Jew or Arab?'*

He told us how he longed for peace and how weary everyone was of war, but said that he felt his people would still have to endure many more years of suffering and deprivation. We stood in silence together, a wise compassionate Muslim and two visitors from the Christian tradition – from a country which in recent years has been involved in much pain in the Middle East. And as we stood in that sacred place, I remembered the great words of Brazil's Bishop Helder Camara: *'Lord, take away from us the quietness of a clear conscience and press us uncomfortably, for only thus that other peace is made, your peace.'*

Minutes after leaving the mosque we were in conversation with a young Palestinian man at a coffee stand on the street. As we drank our rich Arabic coffee, which always leaves its silt in the cup, he told us of the suffering in his village some miles from Bethlehem. A communal suffering which has gone on for years. His people robbed of human dignity at every turning – the victims of sustained oppression. Yet despite it all, he reminded us that the spirit – the soul – of his people would never be destroyed however ground down. He himself, as was obvious, had gone through many deaths of the heart, but his rich humanity and courage shone like a star on that narrow Bethlehem street.

And later, back at the checkpoint into Jerusalem, waiting once again for our passports to be studied and watching the sullen faces of the young security folk, it struck me forcibly what a destructive power fear has in all of our lives. Not just here in Israel/Palestine, but everywhere. And although I find it hard to understand when faced with the mountains of pain which are such a marker in this ancient land, I do believe that God came in Christ, all these centuries ago, not only to reveal our fears but to transform them. To open our being more fully to this extraordinary, often wounded reality which is our human condition. We are not to hide from it, but rather to be aware all the more of these fundamental streams of compassion and of solidarity which reside in us all. In the Palestinian territories the suffering is so obvious, but everyone here – whether Jew and Arab – is in a vortex of pain, and many Israelis long for peace and for a solution to these seemingly intractable problems which in our time disfigure this beautiful land and imprison all its people.

Stevie Krayer is a Quaker of Jewish heritage. Some years ago, she wrote this poem for Jean Zaru, a Palestinian who works ceaselessly for the liberation of her people. For me, this is truly a poem of life, of trust, of hope. It reminds us, in its own tender way, of the One who understands, who weeps with us, and who heals our broken world, and who, all these years ago, was born in the place where I was that afternoon:

> *These days, when I lower my pitcher*
> *into the well, I draw forth*
> *only salt water. I don't see how*
> *our thirst is going to be quenched.*
>
> *Yet I believe the deepest wellspring*
> *remains uncontaminated. This at least*
> *I can do for you, sister,*
> *since I still have tears.*
>
> *While you have wept your eyes*
> *to a dry desolation: weep*
> *on your behalf till the rain*
> *returns and fills the riverbed.*

Glimpses of transformation

During the season of Lent, in the weeks between Ash Wednesday and Easter Sunday, Christians reflect on the inner meaning of the life, death and resurrection of Jesus.

These weeks in the Christian year are a time to ponder not only upon the sufferings of Christ, but also upon contemporary suffering, in our own lives and in the wider world; to renew our efforts to walk alongside the wounded, the frail, the abandoned and the silenced, to become aware in new ways of how the One who holds us all is speaking to us, in a particular way, through their pain. To be reminded that all human suffering is not distant from the heart of God.

Donald Eadie, a valued friend in Birmingham, who himself suffers much pain in his body, has written a beautiful reflection entitled 'The body – wonder and pain, glimpses of transformation'. Donald, who is a former Chair of the Birmingham Methodist District and a wonderful companion to many people, is also the author of *Grain in Winter* (Epworth Press). In recent years, I have recommended this book to many who are seeking a deeper understanding of their faith journey.

Following is an extract from Donald's helpful and challenging reflection:

In earlier years, I took my own body for granted. I was a sportsman, having played both cricket and hockey. In 1994, I developed a degenerative disc disease that has required three major spinal operations and the implanting of scaffolding to support my spine. I had a busy life at the centre of church work and the transition from this to discovering myself as being on the edge was traumatic. I experienced bewilderment, rage and fear – the fear of losing my identity, my role, my relationships: the fear of facing and living with myself, and the fear of the feelings of marginalisation and abandonment.

However, in time, a new sense of vocation has opened up and been lived within the room where I spend so much of my life. I have been drawn more deeply into the paradox within the heart of things: limitation and exploration, contraction and expansion, aloneness and interconnectedness, absence and presence, weakness and strength. I am learning a different way of being within a world obsessed with activity: a vocation to stability with no churchly commissioning. Much of what I reflect upon now is placed in the context of some form of impairment, but I trust that it is much more than that. Frailty and discomfort, wear and tear are natural as our tired bodies age. They belong to the given terrain of the faith journey of older pilgrims …

For many years, Donald has been a member of the Ministry and Disability Group in Birmingham; he writes of his experience within that community:

… We are a fragile yet resilient group. We encourage each other to be real and not heroic, honest and not evasive. Slowly we are learning to live creatively within our reality. We explore a theology of limitation, a vocation to stability, because we recognise that something creative can come from living with both.

We are learning to be laid bare, stripped of roles, responsibilities and masks. Some of us have experienced the humiliation of losing clothes and dignity, being put on bed pans, being taken to the lavatory by others (who in the holy name of Health and Safety must wear gloves), being touched in our nakedness by people we don't know. We share stories of being left unattended in hospital, desperately needing to get to the toilet but being unable to, and then being talked about when the inevitable happens.

Jesus at the end of his life was stripped, stretched horizontal and handed over to others, and is shown as almost naked on the cross. Can we begin to uncover theological and spiritual meaning within this experience of our bodies, our handing over, our being made vulnerable, our being handled by other people? The washing of feet and the stripping of the altars are part of the spirituality of Holy Week. For us, there is need to connect that spirituality of physical weakness and vulnerability with our own experience of weakness.

Some of us in our group experience physical or psychological pain, or both. We live with the mystery that there are those in the world who are 'pain-bearers' and that sometimes some good comes out of all that suffering. We are learning that we can catch glimpses of God in pain. We find ourselves critical of Western medical culture that sees pain as simply something to be got rid of – zapped.

What we have in common is our search for meaning, our search for the resources to live honestly and compassionately within places of darkness, weariness, frustration, pain and vulnerability. For us the group is a 'sacred space' within which we explore the mystery and meaning of our own suffering, where we can tell it as it is for us, where we are able to ponder and listen to the discoveries and insights of others with sublime acceptance and without judgements.

In case all this sounds too pompous and holy, there is something else that is utterly central to our meetings – an infectious vitality and humour. We laugh and laugh, and enjoy a shared experience of leaving the meeting energised and with a deeper hope and trust. This is the group where, above all, we are allowed to be ourselves, and show others who we are.

Prayer

Lord of the pain-bearers,
may I encounter your light in their lives,
and may they continue to illumine our world
as only they can do.

Maundy Thursday

During the years when I had the privilege of working at Iona Abbey, I always felt that Maundy Thursday there was celebrated in an amazingly rich and meaningful way.

We would begin in a crowded Abbey refectory by singing some of the wonderfully relevant and challenging Iona hymns (which now touch hearts around the world), followed by a symbolic washing of feet. Then, in the beauty of that restored room, with its stout walls and glorious roof, we would silently share the bread and the wine. Few words were spoken but the refectory that evening held a thousand emotions.

Then, again in silence, we would make our way down to the dark cloisters to watch a short drama reminding us of the extraordinary events of the day before Jesus was killed. And from the cloisters we slowly walked into the Abbey church.

We stood quietly in the darkness as, one by one, the candles were extinguished and the cross covered or taken away. All was made ready for the morrow: the day on which we would recall the death of Jesus.

And then a total silence enveloped us as we just stood – held in God's wide embrace – and together were caught up in a mystery two thousand years old. And more than once in that great Maundy Thursday silence I heard a pilgrim's tears, reminding me of the mystery and wonder of our human condition.

Some stayed in the Abbey church long into the night, often reflecting not just on themselves but on our beautiful yet violent and divided world.

One by one, we went from that sacred place – permeated with the prayers of the centuries – into the often wild Hebridean night. Our hearts had been moved by a power far beyond ourselves as we re-imagined the events of that first Maundy Thursday. Once again, the fragile yet ever-present Spirit of the One who still suffers so much on our behalf had taken us all into a deeper place. A place articulated in this traditional Gaelic prayer:

> *Each thing we have received,*
> *from you it came, O God.*
> *Each thing for which we hope,*
> *from your love it will be given.*

At home in the dark

At every turn
strange new possibilities
and even stranger uncertainties,
not for the few,
but for us all,
bundled together
in shared confusion.

Waiting and wondering,
sometimes drowning,
hopefully learning.

Learning to be
at home in the dark:
discovering
that the night
brings new horizons
further than the eye can see.

For darkness
also gives birth
to love, to truth,
and to the poet's song,
even if at first we fear
its embrace.

Morning may not quickly come,
but even in the dark
we are
companioned by Light,
and One who is
gently smiling
is calling our name.

Shedding our fears: recognising the face of God

May we disarm our hearts of fear,
and come to that trusting openness
which sees You in every child of God,
and rejoices to welcome You there.

Many years ago I heard this prayer in the States. It has stayed with me ever since because I think it is a resurrection prayer: an Easter prayer for the world, including ourselves. Never has such a prayer been more relevant.

And as we reflect on the beauty and pain of the Easter story, we are reminded that the early followers of Jesus had to shed their fears and come to a trusting openness. The fact that they did so is a miracle in itself. A sign of the Holy Spirit alive in the world, and in human hearts.

On a quite ordinary day, which was to become an extraordinary day, some followers of Jesus encountered a man on the dusty road to Emmaus (Luke 24:13–35). They could not believe that this person had not heard about the cruel death a few days earlier of the one they knew as Jesus. And they talked with this stranger about the event. The conversation went back and forth.

Then the stranger told them some things about his own life.

They walked on further, and came to the village to which they were going. They invited the stranger to stay with them. He came. He sat with them and broke bread. And then their eyes were opened and they recognised who this stranger was. In that simple village home, Jesus was with them. They could shed their fears.

In our utterly divided world, the only way we can walk in trust is through being open to recognising in the stranger in our midst the face of God. And when that perception of 'the other' arises in our heart, we experience again the miracle of that encounter on the Emmaus road.

And around this trust there is a basic question: If we fail to recognise God's presence in the stranger, can we even begin to understand the inner meaning of Easter? For the central meaning of Easter is about unconditional love. God's love for each of us, in every generation. One of the old Jewish tales reminds us that until we recognise in our brother or sister the presence of God, our soul remains in darkness.

It's the ancient yet ever-new invitation to be a person of love, to walk not in fear, but in that trusting openness which comes as a gift to the human heart every day from the heart of God. A truth expressed powerfully in this ancient prayer from the Eastern Orthodox Church:

> *Set our hearts on fire with love to thee, O Christ,*
> *that in that flame we may love thee,*
> *and our neighbour as ourselves.*

Pondering the resurrection body: are there wheelchairs in heaven?

This powerful reflection by Dr Jonathan Inkpin, a friend in Australia, raises many questions:

A few years back, I shared in the Asia Meeting of the Taizé Community in the Philippines, accompanying several young Australians to a wonderful gathering of thousands of Christians from across the Asia-Pacific region. Many aspects of that encounter will continue to enrich and challenge those who took part. One of these was the cultural event on the final afternoon – with songs, dances and other contributions from the people of the different countries represented.

Almost the most memorable was the impressive performance by our three Aboriginal young men, who brought the house down with their songs and dances. However, nothing could compare with the presentation from Japan: One young man took to the stage alone, with his interpreter. A frail, fragile figure, he was curled up awkwardly in a wheelchair, and he spoke haltingly and slurringly, for his motor neuron disease was fairly well-advanced. Yet his words were full of faith and hope, and his joy in Christ put us all to shame. Truly we saw the risen Christ, the wounded healer, shining through him.

When we ponder the risen Christ, what do we see? What are our expectations of the Resurrection, for ourselves and for others? Are we looking for what the world calls 'perfection', or for the glory of our wounded God?

At the same Taizé meeting, I also heard Bishop Kike Figaredo of Cambodia speak. This remarkable Spanish Jesuit has now been involved in Cambodian life for well over 20 years: He runs a rehabilitation centre for the young victims of landmines and cluster bombs and campaigns for the banning of cluster munitions; he has helped Cambodians to reconnect with their obliterated cultural heritage through dance and music; he joyfully fulfils his obligations as the Bishop of Battambang, an area the size of Portugal – and he is also the inventor of the Mekong chair, a special wheelchair for the mine victims, affording them mobility on the dirt tracks in the country. As he himself says, *'Love exists to be transmitted and there are thousands of ways to do so. I do it by being here helping the needy in whatever way I can.'* In doing so, he enables the glory of God to shine through the deep, deep wounds of the Cambodian people.

One of the most startling aspects of the Cambodian Jesuit ministry is its symbol of the mutilated Christ. Missing a limb, like so many Cambodians, the mutilated Christ speaks of the power of God out of profound pain, weakness and destruction. This, and not the 'perfect' bodies of our own culture's vaunted models and sport stars, is the image of the risen Christ, which offers healing and hope to everyone, whoever and wherever we are. Kike Figaredo has been called 'the bishop of the wheelchairs', not only for his work, but also for his teaching of the Gospel. As he himself says, for Cambodians and for others, the wheelchair is a *'sign of hope'*. Indeed, a *'sacrament'*; in a real sense, as with that young Japanese man at the Asia Meeting of Taizé, *'a visible sign of invisible grace'*.

Will there be wheelchairs in heaven? Certainly pain and suffering, tears and mourning will be transformed. Yet, like the risen Christ bearing the saving wounds of his crucifixion, nothing that we have been or borne will ever be lost, in so far as God's glory has shone through it.

As we look at our own wounds, or see others who may at first seem disfigured, may we be blessed by a fresh perception of the risen Christ among us.

Memories

Each year around the anniversary of her death, I visit Dorothy's grave in the small churchyard by the banks of the fast-flowing Spey, in the village of Laggan in Inverness-shire. Close to her grave, friends from the village also lie in that tranquil place. A few of them are very young. Many are older. The graveyard is beautifully kept, and often there are fresh flowers on many of the graves. It is a place of memory for that small Highland community. A sacred place both of sorrow and of light. For many, a place of recollection and of healing:

> In a green place
> of quiet light
> by the waters of the
> fast-flowing Spey,
> watched over by ancient hills
> and gentle woods,
> your body lies
> close by those
> strong church walls
> that held your prayers,
> your songs,
> your laughter
> and inspiring words
> which drew us
> close to God.
> The seasons change
> but still you lie

next to Ian
and Davie
and Margaret
and Peter
and Alastair
and Mary
and Dougal
who, like you,
knew and loved
these ancient
Highland hills,
and called them home.

And when I am there, I often think of many others like myself, around the world, who visit the graves of loved ones. And this year, as I stand amidst the beauty of these Highland hills, I will be remembering those thousands of families who recently have seen their loved ones cut down in acts of violence in many parts of the world. Often brutally murdered because they have dared to raise their voice in defence of basic human rights. And our shared hope is that their agonising deaths will not have been in vain. That from their graves new freedoms for the human spirit and for our common heartbeat will blossom.

In a small booklet of prayers I brought out in remembrance of Dorothy, I included part of a beautiful Gaelic blessing which has given fresh hope to many through the generations:

May the earth be soft under you when you rest upon it,
tired at the end of the day.
And may it rest easy over you when at last you lie under it:
may it rest so lightly over you that your soul may be up
and off from under it quickly,
and on its way to God.

Olive

Shortly after Dorothy's death in 2001, two old friends, Olive and Bill, were staying with me at my cottage in the Highlands. During this visit Olive was involved in a car accident. She died on the spot. Bill was seriously injured, but thankfully recovered.

Why
did it happen,
on that golden
summer's day
on a Highland road
in a place you found so special?

Just moments before,
your life overflowed with
goodness,
wisdom,
expectancy
and love.

Then,
in the twinkling of an eye,
on a sunlit morning
with the one you loved by your side,
you were gone from our midst –
killed by an oncoming car
on the wrong side of the road.

And when I saw
your still body,
I wept,
for in my own grief
you had held me
and spoken words
of gentle hope.
You had shared
my endless tears,
and understood.

And still,
for others
that Highland day was golden,
but my heart was breaking
on that narrow
moorland road.

Remembering

Lord,
you who knew suffering,
may I be still for a moment
and remember
all who today are
silenced
violated
imprisoned
cheated
abused
driven from home
exploited
held hostage
robbed
tortured
rejected
betrayed
marginalised
tyrannised
detained without trial
despised
persecuted
abandoned
killed.

A letter to Fergus

Some years ago when my granddaughter Gabriella had a Blessing Service, I wrote a letter to her. It contained something of my 'theology' and understanding of our connected world.

In 2011, I wrote a letter to Gabriella's young brother, Fergus (then aged two), on the occasion of his Blessing. We often know very little about how our grandparents thought about life. I believe it is important that we know how the generations before us did think, even if our own views are different. Perhaps this reflection can encourage those of us who have grandchildren to write down something (even a little) of how we see the world. This need not be an academic exercise, and if it contains some crazy ideas – all the better. We are all pilgrims on this earth with many dimensions in our lives, and sixty years down the line someone, somewhere may be interested in knowing how we ticked. At least I hope so!

So here is my 'letter to Fergus'. (My grandchildren call me by the nickname 'Apse', which is how I signed this letter.)

Dear Fergus,

It's a good day to be writing you a letter. The day of your Blessing. Long ago when I was young (away back in the time of the Picts) lots of folk sent their grandchildren letters, but in this age of high technology it's much easier to send an e-mail or a text and to make it short. Perhaps you would rather have had an e-mail today: 'Hi Fergus, you sure sound like a cool dude. Love, Apse.'

In a very short time your home will be in Toronto – quite a distance from the quiet lanes of East Bergholt. It won't take you long to discover a basic marker in our globalised world – that we are all interconnected as never before in human history. Given this reality, it is crucial that we never judge others by the colour of their skin, or their religious tradition, or their sexual orientation, or by whether they are rich or poor, or old or young. If our planet is to survive we need one another, and when you are older I hope very much that you will do all in your power to help heal our wounded planet, which today cries out in pain. It is a simple truth that all of life is sacred and precious, not just us human beings who, relatively speaking, have only been around for a short time.

Given the unpredictability both of human life and of our human future, I have been writing in my recent books about some of the qualities we all need in life. I need them. You need them. As you grow up, I would love you to slowly but surely realise that your life is held in God's hands. This means many things. It means we are made in God's image and empowered by the Spirit. It means we affirm God's goodness at the heart of humanity, planted more deeply than all that is wrong. It means that each day we can celebrate the miracle and wonder of life, and the unfolding purposes of God forever at work in ourselves and the world.

Walking in God's light means that people come before possessions – a hard truth in our culture where often what we have matters much more than who we are. It would be wonderful if you could carry in your heart and mind: integrity, compassion and the ability to take risks not just for yourself, but for others. Try not to forget that we live in a global village in which millions of our sisters and brothers are the victims of poverty, war and increasing injustice. And, in a world of many religions, if you do follow the Christian path, I hope you avoid a 'comfortable Christianity' and always believe in a God of surprises who can turn your life upside down.

Be able to laugh at yourself, and at silly jokes; and even if in a few years you strongly believe that your mum and dad know absolutely nothing about life, realise that if you do ever have children of your own, they will, before long, think the same about you! Sometimes that learning process may take sixty years, but hopefully you will get there in the end. This week, I loved reading about a guy who started to grow a ponytail at 85!

Earlier this year I had the privilege of helping with an interfaith book called *Reflections of Life: Words of Comfort and Encouragement.* It was published jointly by the National Health Service and the Scottish government, and copies have gone to all the hospitals in Scotland. Our hope is that the book will bring strength to many people in hospital, whether or not they have faith in God.

I would like to share with you one of my poems from this book. The poem is set in the Highlands of Scotland, where your dad spent some of his teenage years, after returning from living in South India. The words reflect many of the things I believe about life. As you grow up I don't expect you to believe the same things as I do, but I do hope that you will be a person of love, of hope, of sensitivity and of awareness. And if you can – try growing a ponytail at 85!

Highland morning

On this quiet track
in early summer,
amid birch and larch and pine,
who could not sense the sacred
and feel creation's heart of love?

Fourteen centuries have passed since Iona's monks –
at one with nature's pulse,
alive to crag and stream –
trod these Highland hills,
carrying Good News about the One
whose energies of light
pulsate through strath and glen.

This track is holy ground,
a sacred space,
where, walking lightly,
wonder becomes my companion.

I look through the trees
aware of the shy deer
who has grazed here longer than our centuries,
certain heir of mountain and forest.
And as I meet her gaze,
something in my spirit leaps with joy,
for I feel at one with all that lives
on this glorious, Highland day.

Lots of love and go well on your travels. Apse x

A letter to Chloe

My granddaughter Chloe is almost 2 years old. (My grandchildren call me 'Apse'.)

Shanghai, China, May 2012

Dear Chloe,

Thinking of you although I am far away in China. In fact in Shanghai – which the local people here tell me has a population of around 23 million. That makes Edinburgh where I live, with its half a million people, seem like a village. In fact there will soon be 220 cities in China with over one million people in each. And in the whole of China there are 1.4 billion: children, women and men. Can you imagine that? I was thinking about it earlier today – every sixth person on earth lives in this country, and by the time you reach my age that figure will be very much higher.

As you know, our family lived in India for a long time when your dad was young, and some of our friends there had worked as missionaries in China. (Your dad will tell you what a missionary actually is!) These friends told us a lot about China, its people and its long history, but this is my first visit. It is an amazing country and I am sure you will travel here one day. You may even marry a Chinese person, but I am not placing any pressure on you in that regard!

Right now I am writing this letter to you from a small room near the city centre. From my window I can count thirty-seven tall skyscrapers, the tallest one has about seventy storeys. Directly below my window are some of the old, small crowded streets of Shanghai, but every year many of these historic areas are being bulldozed in order to make way for high apartments and offices. I think that is sad but most people think it's progress. I am less certain about that. Certainly the new China is in parts very prosperous – in fact there are now thousands of millionaires in the country. That's a big change from the past. (And by the way, if you become a millionaire don't forget those who struggle for their daily bread!) Here the gulf between poor families and the rich ones is very great, and increasing. It's the same back home.

In the last week I have been travelling a lot by train. Sometimes I have been fourteen hours on the train. The trains always leave exactly on time and arrive on time no matter how far the distance. They carry thousands of passengers. Apart from the regular trains there are also bullet trains and they go very fast between some of the great cities. It's almost like flying but you are on the ground! The trains are also very clean and comfortable, as are the great railway stations here. There is very little litter. Can you believe that, Chloe?

Many things have struck me as I travel here. People are polite and I think there is still a great respect for the elderly, at least in the rural areas. Everyone works long hours and often they have to toil in really dreadful conditions. It's not easy to complain about things here (unlike at home), and if a person complains too much they can be imprisoned. But even this is changing, and many people are demanding fairer wages and better working conditions. Yet it is still the case that any opposition to government policies is not tolerated. When I raised this issue with our Chinese guide she pointed out that while it is difficult to criticise the government in any way, it is also true that the government has raised the standard of living for tens of millions of families. That is true and I see that as I travel around.

I have been to some of the famous tourist sites, like the Great Wall, the Forbidden City and the amazing Terracotta Warriors near Xi'an, but it has also been a real privilege to visit Chinese families in their own homes. Even though we have different cultures and language, we were still able to have a good connection – sharing our humanity, laughing together and enjoying wonderful homecooked food. That's what I like about being in another country – walking alongside ordinary folk who in so many ways are like ourselves, even if their upbringing and history have been hugely different from our own. We all share a common heartbeat, Chloe, and yet we seem to have to go to war with each other, often because we are so certain that our way of life is the 'right way'. There is no 'right way' but *many ways* of living on this small planet. It seems to take us forever to learn that basic truth!

For two days I was with some young Chinese people who are intellectually handicapped. Again we had no common language, but we did have the language of friendship, and when they started to sing a local folk song for me I was in tears. As they sang they began to dance and soon invited me to join them. It was wonderful, and all the cultural differences between us just disappeared in a flash. It was as if I had known these new friends all my life. The room was filled with laughter, acceptance of the other and love. Magic.

After I left these great young people I went to a nearby ancient garden in which people have meditated and found peace in their souls for hundreds of years. These ancient public gardens, scattered all over

103

China, are often places of great beauty with gently flowing water mingling with plants, shrubs, trees and birdsong. They are also places where local families do their daily exercises and share the latest news. For centuries people here have known the inner strength which comes from stilling one's heart and mind, and that is something we are slowly learning about at home as we begin to discover new spiritual paths amidst our frenetic lifestyles.

While most families here are not Christian, I have been surprised by the numbers of people who go to church regularly. Of course this number is small in comparison with the whole population, but it still numbers many millions. For a long time the Christian church in China was persecuted, but it seems (although I may be wrong) that there is now more freedom for worship. Yet there remains a dark side to life here and many citizens are suffering imprisonment and torture for one reason or another. And there is still the death penalty.

In a few days I will be back in Edinburgh. Another kind of world, but in many ways not actually so different. Our world is interconnected as never before, and not just by the Internet. We belong together in this often fragile human family. China is a great nation and its influence in the world is enormous. Yet it is often the small things in our lives that have lasting impact, wherever we belong. Along the street from me here in Shanghai an older man is standing on a small first-floor balcony playing beautiful dance tunes on his saxophone. On the pavement down below literally hundreds of people of all ages are dancing to his music, their faces lit with laughter. The scene is overpoweringly beautiful. A moment of sheer joy on an ordinary street in one of the greatest, most crowded cities on earth. A time just to be. To be human together. That's what brings us hope, Chloe. Hope for our world.

See you soon.

Lots of love from Shanghai!

Apse x

Amidst the washing-up

Be still – and know that I am God (Ps 46:10)

Amidst the washing-up
and shopping
and filling in of forms
and paying bills
and worrying about the next bill
and doing the ironing
and speaking on the phone
and waiting for the bus
and feeding the dog
and paying more bills,
may there be
these moments
of simple awareness
in which
I know I am held
within the wonder of that Love
where my heart
is at home
and at rest.

The connecting of souls

Over the years I have enjoyed collecting prayers from many cultures. As I read them I am aware that at the level of our souls we are deeply connected: to one another, to the Creator of all things and to the good earth upon which we all walk. Despite all our outward differences it is the knowledge of this connecting which enriches our humanity. In being open to 'the other' we become more open to ourselves and to the spiritual path upon which we journey.

I have had the privilege of being in many African countries and love the prayers which are rooted in African spirituality and wisdom. They are prayers for everyday living. Prayers of laughter, of healing, of praise, of penitence, of joy. Often they arise from places of suffering. They always remind us that all of creation sings of the glory of God – every tree, every hill, every river, the beasts of the field and the birds of the air all bear witness to the One who understands all things and who weeps and laughs with us all. Reading these prayers brightens both my heart and my day!:

May the rains fall on our land and the cows grow fat.
May the children take the wisdom of the ancestors
and build upon all that is good.
May time stand still as we gaze upon the beauty that is around us.
May the love in our hearts envelop all those whom we touch.

– A Zulu prayer

The great Rock, we hide behind you.
You are the Great Forest Canopy, giving cool shade:
the Big Tree which lifts its vines to peep at heaven.
You are the Magnificent Tree whose dripping leaves
encourage the luxuriant growth below.
You weave the streams like plaited hair,
and with fountains You tie a knot.

– A prayer by Afua Kuma, who was a farmer and community nurse in northern Ghana; translated from Afua's Twi language by a Jesuit friend

Almighty God,
the All-Seeing Lord up on high who sees
even the footprints of the antelope on a rock mass here on earth,
You are the One who never hesitates to respond to our call.
You are the Cornerstone of Peace.

– An African prayer for world peace

The sun has disappeared.
I have switched off the light,
and my wife and children are asleep.
The animals in the forest are full of fear
and so are the people on their mats.
They prefer the day with Your sun to the night.
But I still know that
Your moon is there,
and Your eyes,

and also Your hands.
Thus I am not afraid.
This day again
You led us wonderfully.
Everybody went to his mat
satisfied and full.
Renew us during sleep,
that in the morning
we may come afresh
to our daily jobs.
Be with our sisters and brothers
far away in Asia
who may be getting up now.

– An evening prayer by a village elder

Coping with illness

Early in 2010, I was diagnosed with major blood clots in my lungs. I had read a lot about clots following Dorothy's very sudden death in March 2001. The clots shooting through Dorothy's body were fatal and her death was instant. I have survived for another day, as they say. Going through this serious illness made me very aware not just of illness itself but of how we find ways to cope when we encounter it.

It would be true to say that most of us hear a great deal about illness: a close friend suddenly faces cancer; an elderly relative moves into the acute stages of dementia; a young man with everything to live for finds himself burdened with depression; a neighbour who has never drunk much in his life and who is physically fit is one day told that his liver is failing; a beautiful young woman studying for her final school exams faces, suddenly, a terminal condition.

Which brings me to my friend Ian who has had severe back pain for many years. Not a day passes for Ian without almost excruciating pain at some point, despite medication. Often during the night this pain continues. It is a constant companion. Yet for all his many friends, Ian is an inspiration – often the first person to contact you if he hears you need a bit of support. In all the years I have known him I have hardly ever heard him complain. His is not a false optimism, for he is well aware that his condition is on a downhill track. But I often think that his attitude, his zest for life and his awareness of others has in some ways lessened his constant background pain. I may be wrong, but it seems that way. His daily journey is hard, and there are many unknowns ahead for him – as there are for all those who carry constant pain in their bodies.

As I write this I am thinking not only about Ian but also about other close friends who are coping with illness at this time. For some of these friends, life is a daily encounter with bodily pain; for others the path is different, as they have moved into that place where ordinary human communication is no longer possible, having entered the deep silence of the mind; for others it is the reality of wrestling with severe depression. In one way or another, each of them is in a place which makes them acutely aware of human vulnerability and physical weakness; and also of our shared mortality and dependence on reliable medical care. I understand a little of this because of that time two years ago when blood clots were moving freely in my own system.

And although it may be trite to say it, we all have different mechanisms for coping. Belief in a God whose love surrounds us has helped millions through the ages to cope with illness, to face it with some degree of serenity. But that ability to cope is also come to by millions of others for whom a faith narrative is not a conscious part of their understanding. And different religious and cultural traditions approach illness and healing in myriad ways.

When I had the privilege of living in a township in South Africa, I was affected deeply by the way in which many of my neighbours who were in the last stages of AIDS encountered their weakness and pain. Time and again I was told by many sick folk: 'We may be dying, Peter, but you know something – today we are *living*!' 'Today we are living' is a phrase that often comes back to me. It is such a powerful truth, even in the face of great human suffering. And along with that truth, I witnessed in South Africa another truth – that illness often (though not always) allows us to see the amazing courage of the human spirit.

111

That is not for a moment to say that we need illness to understand more clearly our human condition, but it is to reaffirm that our essential humanity is sometimes enlarged through suffering. This in itself is a difficult spiritual and theological issue, and not all would agree that illness can enable us to enter into a deeper humanity. Many don't cope calmly with illness and because of it become angry, frustrated and cynical about life. And that too we can easily understand, for facing illness is never a clear-cut path – even for those who outwardly appear to live with acceptance of infirmity of body or mind.

Yet as we think about this whole issue of coping with illness, I hope we can be consciously experiencing that somewhere, someone is walking with us. Actually walking with us – at the level of our depths. Over the years in my pastoral work, I have seen that illness carried alone is truly a bleak journey. Even if we have only one other person understanding what we are going through it's worth a million bucks.

Many of those who visit the island of Iona have found meaning in the weekly Service of Prayers for Healing held in the Abbey. People of all faiths and none have shared in prayers for those who are sick either in mind or in body, and I myself find hope and healing in the simple words of the final blessing:

> *God to enfold you.*
> *Christ to touch you.*
> *The Spirit to surround you.*

Known, yet unknown

Known, yet unknown,
without a name,
yet holding every name.

In the mystery of love
you come to us
and in tenderness reveal
the meaning of our lives
and the pattern of our days.

*Inspired by some words of Albert Schweitzer
in The Quest of the Historical Jesus*

Mike's note

Mike is a friend, whose sister, Lynda, died from cancer when she was 19. He is a searcher after truth, and a person of compassion – and he would be devastated if he could not play his weekly football match!

Dear Peter,

When I met you the other day, you asked about my work as a volunteer at the local hospice for folk with cancer. I wanted to tell you more, but had to get back to the office.

Lynda, my sister, was 19 when she died in this same hospice. I hated the place at first, and did not want Lynda to go. But I've changed. I used to be a total fitness freak, then when I saw Lynda's body going away – she was a good swimmer – I began to think differently. Our bodies don't seem to matter all that much; it's what's inside.

Some months after Lynda died I went back to the hospice to say 'hello' to some of the staff – I think they are magic. Before I knew what I was saying I said that I'd come as a volunteer. And I did – much to my own surprise!

At the hospice, no one forces themselves on you. You come and go – and there is always a welcome. You can be yourself. It's peaceful, and they don't preach at you. I do odd jobs. After a couple of weeks, I began to get close to some of the patients. One of them thinks of me as her 'toy boy' and we joke around.

Next year I'll be 25. I've new directions, and would like to go into social work. I think more people my age should offer themselves as volunteers.

They asked me to go and speak with a guy – same age as myself. He was so sick. It was hard, but now he looks forward to seeing me. I don't think he'll be around for long.

I miss Lynda and try to support mum and dad. I sometimes think about religion. We've never had anything to do with it, but one of the chaplains took Lynda's funeral, and it was nice. He seemed like a regular bloke. He was a friendly guy and seemed to know what we were going through. After the funeral he gave me a hug. Just gave me a hug and said nothing. Now I do that myself to some of these folk in their beds at the hospice. It's all you can do sometimes.

Cheers,

Mike

P.S. Still out there on the pitch on Saturdays!

Listening

'Listening is the highest form of love.'

These words were written by the late, well-known theologian Paul Tillich. A simple yet powerful truth.

Amid our endless words and chatter may we possess that gift of the spirit, the gentle art of listening: both to our own inner voice and to that precious – and often hidden – voice in the other person.

To really hear what the other person is saying is a work of love, of acceptance, of wisdom.

> *God of deep quiet,*
> *still my soul,*
> *my heart,*
> *my mind,*
> *that I may listen*
> *in such a way that*
> *my listening*
> *in itself*
> *becomes*
> *an act of love.*

Profiles in courage

Luc Besson's film *The Lady* tells the incredible story of Aung San Suu Kyi of Burma (now Myanmar) who millions of us around the world regard as one of the truly great people of our time. It not only tells her story but also poignantly shows what the Burmese people have suffered since 1962, when the country became a brutal – unbelievably brutal – military dictatorship. It is a film about human courage and fearlessness in the face of unrelenting oppression.

Back in 1990 Aung San Suu Kyi's National League for Democracy (NLD) won 81% of the seats in Parliament, but the dictatorship refused to budge, and since then, more or less continually, she has been under house arrest in Rangoon, facing constant death threats. The suffering of many of those who supported the NLD is beyond description, and even today the UK Burma Campaign estimates that there are at least 1,000 political prisoners languishing in prisons which can only be described as hellholes. In the years since 1990, tens of thousands of ordinary children, women and men have been slaughtered.

In this nightmare situation Aung San Suu Kyi has been a light for basic human rights and freedoms – an inspiration not only for her own suffering people but for every human being who believes in human dignity. In our world of false celebrity, she truly is a person we can all respect – and one day she will lead her people to lasting freedom.

A life such as hers raises many questions. How is it possible for a human being to endure so much torment on a daily basis, and for years on end, and still remain a person of such compassion, serenity and awareness?

What is the kind of hope such a person carries within their heart and mind? How can such a life of self-sacrifice influence our own lives in a world so concerned with the self? Are such people who live out the way of non-violence in the world enabling us all to enter more deeply into our shared humanity?

Aung San Suu Kyi's books, including *Letters from Burma* and *Freedom from Fear,* give us some understanding of her life, which is earthed in daily, disciplined meditation and in the belief that everyone is precious. As her own behaviour makes clear, she has moved beyond fear and is convinced that fear should never prevent us from doing what we know to be right. For her *'it is not power that corrupts but fear. Fear of losing power corrupts those who wield it …'* (From *Freedom from Fear*)

Wherever we may be in the world, the people of Burma need our support and it would be good if we could all be in touch with local campaigns for the freedom of its people. The British website for the Burma Campaign is www.burmacampaign.org.uk. There is also a similar campaign in the States. As Aung San Suu Kyi always makes clear, it is not just her we should be concerned about it, but much more the millions of ordinary families throughout Myanmar who suffer so much. The future of the country is still far from clear and even basic democracy a long way off …

Early in 2012, Stephen Hawking, the great theoretical physicist, who since the age of 22 has lived with motor neuron disease, celebrated his 70th birthday. In a tribute to him, his friend Lord Rees, the Astronomer Royal, said:

'... He has become arguably the most famous scientist in the world, acclaimed for his brilliant research ... and, above all, for his astonishing triumph over adversity ...

The concept of an imprisoned mind roaming the cosmos has grabbed people's imagination ... And what a triumph his life has been so far. His name will live in the annals of science; millions have had their cosmic horizons widened by his best-selling books; and his unique achievement against all the odds is an inspiration to even more.'

It is almost impossible to comprehend the physical struggles which Stephen Hawking has had to overcome in the past 50 years. Yet as his body became frailer, his work has enabled us to understand the cosmos in totally new ways. How is it possible? All we know is that it has been possible, and for that the world is grateful. We cannot read of Stephen Hawking's life without being deeply inspired ...

Eighteen years ago, a young black man was murdered at a bus stop in London. His name was Stephen Lawrence, and in all the years since then, his mother, Doreen Lawrence, and his father, Neville Lawrence, have fought to bring the killers to justice. That has now happened with the conviction of Gary Dobson and David Norris.

The Stephen Lawrence case has changed many things in Britain – and changed them for the good – and behind it all shines the incredible courage of the Lawrences over these long years. They did not give in – against all the odds. The struggle to bring justice for Stephen has brought them personal sorrow and mountains of stress and anxiety. You can see that etched clearly in the face of his mother Doreen. It has also, sadly, cost them their marriage.

Many of us have followed this titanic struggle for justice over the years. Here was a loving, ordinary family thrust into a nightmare which went on and on. But their human dignity has shone through it all, and their enormous courage in the face of endless closed doors. Those in places of power refused to listen, but had to in the end. In their determination not to give up, the Lawrences, without malice, have changed many aspects of race relations in this country.

The Lawrences and Stephen Hawking and Aung San Suu Kyi allow me to understand a little more about the human spirit, and about the depths of that spirit at work within us all.

Prophets of truth

They are not strangers,
those who today oppose tyrants
and corruption in high places.

Nor are they faceless ones,
those who walk with death
to gain our accustomed freedoms.

They are not
'an enemy within' –

but witnesses to truth,
illumining multiple falsehoods
amidst the dark places of modernity.

And in their courage we can encounter
something deep within ourselves:
the tender voice of solidarity.

For in their quest for justice,
and in their songs for freedom,
they are prophets of truth –
ordinary folk,
our sisters and brothers –
humbly reminding us
of what it means to be human
amidst the fragile glitz of affluence.

A life of beauty

Kharbibi Mohammed, who lives in Souk Labbadine in Marrakesh in Morocco, is not well-known. In fact only a handful of people know this 64-year-old woodcarver. Recently I met him in Spain, by chance, as he was carving – using traditional tools – some of the most beautiful boxes, trays and bowls I have ever seen. Kharbibi's work in thuya, sandal and lemonwood, sometimes inlaid with silver, could easily be displayed in our national galleries.

In his quiet, unobtrusive way he reminds us of a basic fact: that without beauty our world is truly impoverished – true beauty that comes from hundreds of years of knowledge that has been handed down through the generations. Not the cheap beauty to which we are accustomed. Something quite different. An artist who seeks not his or her own glory produces, in my book, truly beautiful things. Works of art that touch the soul. And their work is often rooted in personal struggle, in a genuine humility and in an inner spiritual journey which is not made public.

Kharbibi's tools are unbelievably traditional, and I asked myself: How can such basic tools, hardly changed with the centuries, craft such amazingly beautiful work? They do. And in his own way, Kharbibi is passing his incredible skill to the next generation. What a tragedy for the world if such unique craftsmanship was to disappear.

As I talked to him, with the help of a Muslim friend who speaks Arabic, I felt that I was with a 'great soul': someone who had experienced the depths and heights of life – yet each day spent hours with his tools creating beauty for others. Kharbibi has enlarged my vision – his is a life embedded not in power, status and wealth, but in realities quite different: genuine creativity, faithfulness to the task and integrity of spirit. Qualities of the soul which are easily abandoned in our present culture.

The state visit of Pope Benedict to the UK, 2011

We who are charged with announcing the message of Christ need to learn the incomparable lesson that he taught us by his own example. He taught first of all with his life and only then did he preach.

— Dom Helder Camara of Brazil

The church looks at the world with profound understanding, with sincere admiration, and with the sincere intention not of dominating it, but of serving it; not of despising it, but of appreciating it; not of condemning it, but of strengthening and saving it.

— Pope Paul VI, in 1963

In 2011 the Pope paid a state visit to Britain. It is estimated that up to 500,000 people saw him in person during his four-day trip. Many of the good and great shook his hand, and the Queen gave him a cup of tea in her official Edinburgh residence, the ancient palace of Holyrood, which is adjacent to a former monastic foundation. And over and above all of this, perhaps a billion people worldwide saw something of his visit on their televisions.

Within an hour of his arrival in Scotland, where the official visit began, and standing alongside the monarch, the Pope launched into an attack on *'atheist extremism'*. He reminded his Edinburgh and worldwide audience that *'aggressive secularism'* is embedded in British society, and that the exclusion of God, religion and virtue from public life has done incomparable damage in the last century. The need for the Christian voice to be heard and listened to in the public arena was a central theme in all of his many speeches in Britain.

His pronouncements brought criticism from secularists and some religious groups. Terry Sanderson, the president of the National Secular Society in the UK, said: *'The British people have embraced a secular identity of their own free will, perhaps as a reaction to the ultra-conservatism of this present papacy and the extremism that has been manifested by some forms of Islam. The secular identity of the British people is not something to criticise, but to celebrate.'*

Personally I feel that the Pope's speeches do raise fundamental questions for society. This is a long-term debate, and not just in Britain. Many people are writing about it and raising these important questions for public debate:

How do we understand the word 'secular'?

Is it true to say (as many in fact do say) that people in Britain who profess a faith in Christ feel marginalised and misunderstood by society at large?

Have Christians themselves, by their silence and/or by their respect for a secular identity, contributed to these feelings of marginalisation?

What does it mean to say that the churches should be 'heard'?

What of the role of faith schools?

Should there be any religious articulation in political life?

In England should there still be 'an established Church'?

What do we actually mean by a 'plural' or 'multicultural' society? What do we mean by 'embracing diversity'?

How do we retain mutual respect and understanding in a society of such diversity? Is that possible?

Where are the forums for such discussions?

What is your own view of Christianity within a secular society?

Was Pope Benedict's understanding of secularism right?

The writer Brendan Walsh, who believes, as I do, that there are hopeful signs in secular society – even as we acknowledge its flaws, failures and uncertainties – says:

> *There are arguments to be had about the underlying values and quality of contemporary culture but no one, surely, can fail to recognise that it is immensely varied and complicated. Beside the hopelessness and despair there is moral seriousness, a desire to find the good life in a confusing and brutal world. It is in many ways a more thoughtful, kinder culture, more concerned about injustice and discrimination than any before it. Traditional theology and philosophy may have run out of steam but people are discovering the sacred in new and unexpected spaces, in work for social justice, in new kinds of commitment and public ritual. Alongside the dreary repetition, the dross and kitsch of contemporary culture, there is plenty of surprise and invention. Fusions and cross-fertilisations of different ethnic traditions and especially the impact of new communications technologies have stirred up the cultural gene pool. It is interesting out there. Intelligent listening, sifting and discernment would be welcome.*

Brendan Walsh, from an article in *The Tablet*, March 1996

In this present moment:
the wisdom of the Dalai Lama

Recently I had the privilege of listening to the Dalai Lama during his visit to Edinburgh. The Usher Hall, one of the largest concert halls in the city, was packed with people of all ages. After his talk, young people from local schools asked him many questions. He also presented an award for compassion to a 17-year-old Edinburgh school pupil who has done much to raise awareness about schizophrenia, from which her mother suffers.

Some Christians feel that we cannot learn anything from other religious traditions. For me that only leads to a real impoverishment of the soul. The years I spent in India, a country where several faith traditions exist side by side, gave me a great appreciation of other pathways to the divine, a deeper spiritual awareness and understanding. The late and much mourned Bede Griffiths, one of the great spiritual voices of our time, was right when he said that living in India had allowed him to discover *the other half of his soul*.

I have always admired the Dalai Lama. For 70 years he has been in public life. He has endured all kinds of human sorrow and for decades has been harshly condemned by one of the largest nations on earth, yet he remains a man of extraordinary compassion, humour, wisdom and light. No wonder that in our often spiritually bankrupt Western countries, thousands flock to listen to his words and to be inspired by his example of selfless love. He does not preach, but makes clear we share the quest for a more compassionate humanity.

Throughout the world the Dalai Lama, although himself a Buddhist, addresses the fundamental question of a secular ethic for modern societies. A question also addressed today by Christian theologians, such as Hans Küng in Germany. How do we live with moral values, with compassion, with a greater awareness of our interconnectedness in a world which is often subject to, if not controlled by, technology?

He does not speak in the abstract or in terms of doctrine. He begins with where we are as humans: often bewildered; often seeking to do good but in that very doing being misunderstood; often under stress in our personal relationships; often carrying various forms of grief; often afraid of the future; often blaming some kind of god for what goes wrong; often falling into addiction because reality may be too harsh to face.

Given all these many voices clamouring for attention in our minds, the Dalai Lama says that mindfulness is therefore crucial. Being aware of the moment and of what that moment holds. Not the past, nor the future, but this present time which may carry within it both joy and sorrow, pain and laughter. As we say in the Christian tradition: *'This is the day which the Lord has made: let us rejoice and be glad in it.'* Not some other day – but *this* day. *This* hour, *this* moment. The only moment in which we are actually present.

And in this present moment, can we encounter reality with a mind which is not constantly wavering and restless, but rather accepting the moment for what it is?: A time to live wisely and fully. To accept our vulnerability along with our strengths. To live calmly with the fact that life is short and that much of it is mystery. To be able to be joyful knowing that we have many more questions than answers and that the opposite of faith is not doubt but certainty.

In a part of the Buddha's teachings we read this:

Cast off selfishness, false desire, hatred and greed but cherish faith, watchfulness, energy, contemplation and vision.

It would be a truly impoverished soul who did not discover both wisdom and challenge in such words. And wise souls in every religious tradition enable us to grow spiritually and to live serenely. That is why the One who holds us all put them in our midst on earth, not just in heaven.

A trip to Staffa

If you look up the island of Staffa on Wikipedia, you read and find this information:

Staffa (Gaelic: Stafa), from the Old Norse for stave or pillar, is an island in the Inner Hebrides in Scotland. The Vikings gave it this name as its columnar basalt reminded them of their houses, which were built from vertically placed tree logs. Staffa lies about 10 kilometres (6.2 miles) west of the isle of Mull. The area is 33 hectares (0.13 square miles), and the highest point is 42 metres (138 feet) above sea level. It is of volcanic origin and is around 55-58 million years old. It is the nesting place for large groups of puffins, black-legged kittiwakes, the common shag and gulls. In the waters around the island, at various seasons, are grey seals, dolphins, basking sharks and minke and pilot whales.

The gigantic sea cavern on Staffa, which was named by the explorer Sir John Banks in the late 18th century, is known as 'Fingal's Cave', and it was the sound of the rushing waves within this incredible natural phenomenon which inspired Mendelssohn to compose his Hebridean Overture. *The sea cavern also, it seems, delighted Queen Victoria on her visit.*

Over the years Staffa has been visited by literally thousands of people from around the world, and it is regarded as one of the great natural wonders in the British Isles. It lies close to the sacred island of Iona, where St Columba established his monastery in 563 and which today is the spiritual home of the Iona Community.

For the last thirty-five years, a good friend of mine, Davie Kirkpatrick, who lives on Iona, has been taking visitors to Staffa in his small but sturdy boat, the *Iolaire*. The round trip lasts about three hours and that includes around an hour on the island, if the conditions are favourable for landing.

Not long ago I had the privilege of being with Davie and a few others, including my cousin Liz and her husband, Sandy, on the Staffa trip. It was a Saturday afternoon with wonderful Hebridean sunshine above us and fairly choppy seas beneath us. In fact you could say it was a rough sea, especially on our return journey through the beautiful Sound of Iona – where we saw a basking shark and grey seals and their pups enjoying the early-evening sunshine.

On every trip, Davie spends time talking with the folk on his boat. He is a fund of information on every topic imaginable, and not just on local knowledge, and is also a good listener. His stories are limitless and full of real delight! Many of those who have sailed on the *Iolaire* to Staffa (even if the sea has been choppy) arrive back on the Iona jetty both refreshed and renewed. Time and again people have told me that it was not just a trip to a famous island, but also a healing experience in which they could have time to reflect upon their life. That experience is also helped by the magnificence of the natural beauty in this area of the Inner Hebrides.

Davie and his wife, Carol, have known personal sorrow. In 1998 their only son, Davie, was drowned on a December evening in the Sound of Iona. Three other young men from the village community on Iona were also drowned along with him. It was a huge tragedy for the folk on Iona and on neighbouring Mull, and it was several weeks before all four bodies were washed onto various shores. For all of us who shared in Iona's grief during that dark December it was *'a time outside time'*, as one of the other grieving parents said to me the night before the first funeral following the drownings, that of young Robert Hay.

Many years earlier, in the 1950s, Davie Kirkpatrick's dad, Charlie, had been killed in an accident on the island when he was working, along with many others, on the restoration of the monastic buildings at Iona Abbey. At that time, Davie was only a young lad, one of the Kirk-patricks who have lived on Iona for many generations.

I mention these two deaths in Davie and Carol's family because I know that these sorrows have enabled both of them, in their own ways, to be able to walk alongside hundreds of others who have met them on the boat or on Iona, and who have experienced loss and troubles in their own lives.

This kind of interconnected, aware and everyday spirituality of hope and of welcome, never expressed in some pious religious language, I find inspiring. It comes from the heart and speaks to the heart. Folk like Davie and Carol would be the last people in the world to claim that in their daily work they are engaged in a 'ministry' but in my understanding it is that – in the best sense of the word. We have all met such people on our journey through life; they may live on our street or be behind the counter in our local store, and it is a gift from God that we can be touched and affected by their quiet, unobtrusive spirituality.

A few hundred yards from the small Iona jetty where visitors board Davie's welcoming Staffa-bound boat stands the magnificently restored and world-famous Iona Abbey. Thousands visit the Abbey each year, and huge numbers of people from every continent share in its ongoing, daily worship. Some briefly, others for longer, depending upon their time on the island. In that ancient place of prayer, the ecumenical Iona Community, which is committed to a Christianity which engages with the modern world, reminds us that we are all *made in the image of God, befriended by Christ and empowered by the Spirit*.

The Community also reminds us, through its work and worship in the world, *to affirm God's essential goodness at the heart of all of humanity, planted more deeply than all that is wrong, and to celebrate the miracle and wonder of daily life*. That is inspiring, even to those who find belief in God difficult.

The Community also speaks about *the unfolding purposes of God, forever at work in ourselves and the world*. If we live unaware of the signs of these unfolding purposes we are spiritually impoverished. These signs are present everywhere. And on Iona they are seen not just in an ancient but living Abbey, but also in a small boat heading for Staffa, sometimes in choppy, rain-soaked seas, and sometimes companioned by grey seals and dancing dolphins. With perhaps a puffin flying overhead.

Revolutions in our time

What is happening throughout the Arab world affects us all. As I write this in the summer of 2012, Syria is in flames. In its towns and cities many are dying daily. We watch the plumes of thick black smoke rising after a bomb explosion on some crowded street in Damascus and silently wonder how many local folk have perished in an instant. And this bleak scenario of destruction is being mirrored across the Arab world. Everywhere people who have felt oppressed for generations are seeking to break free from their chains.

We cannot sit back. For those who seek new freedoms are not strangers but our sisters and brothers who through no fault of their own have found themselves living under oppressive regimes of one kind or another. There is a line in a poem from Tunisia which is being chanted in demonstrations throughout the Arab world: *'When the people decide to live, destiny will obey and chains will be broken.'* Yet as these chains are being severed, terrible human suffering becomes embedded in daily living. Can it be otherwise when tyrants refuse to hear the voices of the people?

The Palestinian poet Mourid Barghouti, writing in *The Guardian* about these revolutions, quoted from one of his poems: *Nothing goes off suddenly; even the earthquakes set in motion from the depths of the earth to the rooftops of the villages.'* The revolutions in our time may look new, but the groundwork for them goes back many years; they will not have happened suddenly, even if it seems like that to the outside observer. The cries of the people have been silenced for too long. The silenced are waking.

This is both a political and a spiritual issue. At its core is the question of human rights, which is inseparably bound up with the issue of justice. Sadly, some Christians see the quest for basic rights as having nothing to do with their faith, which led Desmond Tutu many years ago to ask: *'Which Bible are these folk reading?'*

We who read about all of this are not, thankfully, living under Arab-style dictatorships. We may complain about the proliferation of CCTV cameras, but hopefully we do not yet have secret police watching our movements. Yet given the fact that we have such a range of freedoms should we not be actively concerned about those in our world who have so few? We are linked to their hopes and struggles, as Christian Aid and many other charities make clear. These cries for human dignity are not taking place on another planet but on this one – the one we all share. I often think of that wise old saying from a Chinese Christian, which is as relevant as ever: *'The real atheism is to exclude God from our worldly concerns, or to exclude the world from our religious concerns.'*

Far beyond the Arab world, in Asia and in Africa, we see ordinary people beginning to question the oppressive, corrupt structures which they have endured for generations. In the villages of South India, some of which I know well, violation of basic human rights continues to be a daily reality for millions of Dalit (formerly named Untouchable) families. And in these rural communities the upper castes do all in their power, including murder, to retain the status quo. In such situations to say there is basic justice for the poorest is a cruel joke. And surely God must weep over such forms of oppression, which are made even worse by the fact that in the same country millions of families are better off than ever before.

Inevitably this widespread turmoil brings many fears in its trail. Is the human family destined to be in a permanent state of chaos and of revolt? Can anyone on earth be actually 'secure'? Is our 'way of life' disappearing forever? What kind of world will our grandchildren inherit? What part is religion playing in it all? Is the gulf between poor and rich just going to get wider and wider? Have our new technologies, while opening up many possibilities to millions, actually made daily living tougher for millions of others? Have our globalised markets plunged whole nations into even greater poverty?

To these questions some will reply, 'It has always been so.' Wars and rumours of wars, famine, oppression and destitution have always been part of the human condition. Some will tell us to keep calm as there is nothing new in human history. The subjugation of millions by a single, ruthless individual has been a marker of the human story. And much of the Old Testament is itself a witness to brutal dehumanising realities. And does it surprise us, as we look at all of this chaos and death, that many folk come to the conclusion that there is no God, that, for better or worse, we are alone in this human drama?

Yet there is another truth at work in all of this. I learned about it first-hand in India. It's a simple truth: God, often weeping, is at the heart of the people's struggles. I saw this understanding of God also in the townships of South Africa as folk there battled with AIDS and unemployment. In the 1980s thousands of suffering families in Latin America believed that God's power was with them in their struggles for liberation. That in a profound sense, God was the liberator – guiding them through their confrontations with tyrants.

The present revolutions in many countries have a long journey ahead. A journey involving suffering, betrayals and dashed hopes. But through it all our prayer is that one day human freedoms will flourish. Yet for those of us who try to walk the path of faith, the question remains: Is God standing idly by, or there in the midst of it all?

There is no easy answer to that, but for me this Labourer's Creed, which came out of the struggles for human dignity in Latin America, is a signpost. An illuminator. Over the years these words have helped me to believe that God has not abandoned us. For God the liberator is also the One who calls for justice on the face of this good earth.

I believe
in a God who shares with us
the thorny ground
and all the uninviting places
where some of us have to live.
In a God
who suddenly weeps floods of tears,
with hands outstretched like a mother,
over my red and black village.

I believe in a God
who never lets go from one struggle to the next.
A friend who is there with me
from coffee at daybreak
until I sleep at night.

'Jesus is coming – look busy!'

Lord,
I like these fun words on my friend's fridge door,
but is it true that I have to look busy when you're around?

I'm always busy, and I thought that at least when you came,
there would be time to talk, have a drink, relax,
and maybe watch TV.

For I once read that when you were visiting two sisters,
one of them just sat at your feet, lay back,
and did nothing but listen to your words.
And you told her that was OK.

So maybe it's OK to watch TV together,
and have a beer when you come round.

Let me know. See you soon.

Planted more deeply than all that is wrong

During the last few years in the Iona Community we have used an Affirmation of Faith, words which reassure me when all around looks fairly bleak. Or very bleak! The words in this affirmation are simple, yet I know that they help me to refocus, to calm my spirit, to see the wider picture and to believe that my journey has meaning.

Part of this affirmation contains these lines:

> With people everywhere
> WE AFFIRM GOD'S GOODNESS
> AT THE HEART OF HUMANITY,
> PLANTED MORE DEEPLY THAN ALL THAT IS WRONG.

At one level this is a magnificent proclamation of God's essential goodness permeating the very core of our human story. It reminds me of that soaring passage in Paul's letter to the Christians in Rome, at the end of Romans chapter 8, and here I put it in my own words: *'We have, even on bleak days, this truth: that nothing can separate us from God's love, neither death nor life, not a single thing in all creation will be able to take from us the tender compassion of the One who made and holds us all.'*

That seems to be saying to me that when all the chips are down this divine power of love is embedded in the human fabric in such a way that the accumulated ills and wrongs of the centuries are never the final word. That there is always and everywhere 'another word' – one which is not about hatred or violence or betrayal. A word which enables us to discover who we truly are in our shared humanity. A goodness which cannot be extinguished, and which threads through our common heart-beat. A goodness which enables us to recognise that the very ground we walk on is holy, is good, is blessed. Is of God.

And when I am asked about what it means to have faith in Christ, I come back to these words in the affirmation which I believe sum up a truth which is at the core of the Christian message. This goodness is not an abstract idea but resides wherever love wins over hatred; hope over fear; truth over cruel lies. Truly goodness is planted more deeply than all the evil. Yet we often only understand that truth as we learn to accept the broken, ugly bits in ourselves. The vulnerabilities, the failures, the easy turning to self-pity. The sheer lack of goodness!

As I have grown older I have become more conscious within myself of two realities, which at first may seem contradictory. The first is my recognition that I carry within me a lot of brokenness and many unhealed memories. The second is that even when I feel burdened and bewildered, I also 'feel held'. I know that I am not the only person to feel like this! In other words, there is a goodness working its way through the tangled layers of awareness in me, even if I am unable to define it in an exact way. And somewhere, deep inside me, I also believe this goodness to be at work in the life of the world – a world which bears witness to numberless cries of pain.

Eddie Askew, who worked tirelessly for The Leprosy Mission, wrote many beautiful prayers, one of which had this line in it: *'Lord in you is strength, however contrary the tide.'* That is such a tender and encouraging insight into the energies of God. An insight which reaffirms for us this working out of goodness in all things; through all of time and through the vast tapestry of human drama. And what helps me to go on when days are hard is that it's a goodness seeping through the cracks of everyday life, appearing again and again in the very places which we do not imagine would be touched by God's surprises. But which in fact are.

Not lost or in despair

One truth of our times:
for us all
the journey is uncertain –
rich in uncharted paths and hidden mines
which easily arouse our silent fears.

So we are hesitant, and hope the storm will pass.
Yet we are not immune from global pain,
and share a common fate on fragile earth.
A 'fate', we say, but is it only that,
as we survey the strangeness of our age
and feel embedded in discomfort?

Have we ditched hope
and life-giving ways of understanding?
Of seeing new paradigms amidst the gales
and learning once again to sing and dance?

We are not lost, or in despair –
for everywhere are signs of Light
when we have eyes to see
and the gift to free ourselves from ourselves.

This is a new day –
and One who knows beyond our knowing
is closer than we think.

A time to mend

Through
hunger,
injustice,
poverty,
violence,
and the other
sorrow-filled markers
of our age,
there is a time
to pause,
to listen,
to laugh,
to see beauty,
to seek truth,
to love deeply,
and to mend our broken
but beautiful
human fabric.

And maybe,
just maybe,
that time is
now –
today,
right where we are.

Go gently

Go gently, my friends:
feel the good earth beneath your feet,
celebrate the rising of the sun,
listen to the birds at dawn,
walk gently under the silent stars,
knowing you are on holy ground.

Sources and acknowledgements

Affirmation from the morning service in Iona Abbey – by Philip Newell, Neil Paynter and Brian Woodcock, *Iona Abbey Worship Book*, Wild Goose Publications, 2001 © Iona Community

'The pilgrim path' – from *An Iona Prayer Book*, Peter Millar, Canterbury Press, 1998. © Peter Millar 1998. Used by permission of Peter Millar.

'Challenging God' – from *The Surprise of the Sacred: Finding God in Unexpected Places*, Peter Millar, Canterbury Press, 2004. © Peter Millar 2004. Used by permission of Peter Millar

'We need not only have moralism or despair ...' – from *The Kingdom Is Theirs: Five Reflections on the Beatitudes*, Rowan Williams, Christian Socialist Movement, 2002

'Aids is so limited ...' – from *African Women, HIV/AIDS and Faith Communities*, Phiri, Isabel A. Haddad; Beverley & Masenya, Madipoane (eds.), Cluster Publications, 2005

'We cannot escape our grief or the losses we have experienced ...' – from *Witness to AIDS*, Edwin Cameron, I.B. Tauris, 2005, p.214

'Guru Nanak and truthful living' – from *The Surprise of the Sacred: Finding God in Unexpected Places*, Peter Millar, Canterbury Press, 2004. © Peter Millar 2004. Used by permission of Peter Millar

'Lord, Thou bestowest love ...' – Govind Singh, in *God of a Hundred Names: Prayers and Meditations from Many Faiths and Peoples*, Barbara

Greene and Victor Gollancz (eds), Littlehampton Book Services Ltd, 1962

'Thankfully, but often slowly, we are awakening to the acceptance of difference' – from *Waymarks: Signposts to Discovering God's Presence in the World*, Peter Millar, SCM-Canterbury Press, 2000

'As I come to a mellow, even peaceful awareness …' – from *Waymarks: Signposts to Discovering God's Presence in the World*, Canterbury Press, 2000. © Peter Millar 2000. Used by permission of Peter Millar

'With just 361 words …' – from 'A Nation Apologies', by Phillip Coorey and Stephanie Peatling, *The Sydney Morning Herald*, February 13, 2008

'The hovering spirit' – from *The Surprise of the Sacred: Finding God in Unexpected Places*, Peter Millar, Canterbury Press, 2004. © Peter Millar 2004. Used by permission of Peter Millar

'For Aboriginal people …' – David Tacey, from *Re-enchantment: the New Australian Spirituality*, David Tacey, Harper Collins, 2000

'An alder leaf, loosened by wind, is drifting out with the tide …' – from *The Spell of the Sensuous*, David Abram, Vintage Books, 1997, p.274

'These days, when I lower my pitcher …' – from the poem 'Via Dolorosa', Stevie Krayer. Used by permission of Stevie Krayer. This poem first appeared as the epigraph to *When the Rain Returns: Toward Justice and Reconciliation in Palestine and Israel* (prepared by an international Quaker Working Party on Israel and Palestine, 2004), American

Also by Peter Millar ...

Good News of Great Joy: Daily Readings for Advent from Around the World (with Neil Paynter), Wild Goose Publications

Light of the World: Daily Readings for Advent (with Neil Paynter), Wild Goose Publications

Our Hearts Still Sing: Daily Readings, Wild Goose Publications

We Journey in Hope: Reflections on the Words from the Cross (with Neil Paynter), Wild Goose Publications

An Iona Prayer Book, Canterbury Press

Finding Hope Again: Journeying Through Sorrow & Beyond, Canterbury Press

Iona: A Pilgrim's Guide, Canterbury Press

The Surprise of the Sacred: Finding God in Unexpected Places, Canterbury Press

Waymarks: Signposts to Discovering God's Presence in the World, Canterbury Press

Campfires and Wellsprings in Unexpected Places (with Anne McPherson) Wellspring Community, Australia (www.wellspringcommunity.org.au)

Letters from Madras, CLS, India

Peter Millar blogs at: http://petermillarreflects.blogspot.co.uk/

Wild Goose Publications is the publishing house of the Iona Community, which is:

- An ecumenical movement of men and women from different walks of life and different traditions in the Christian church

- Committed to the gospel of Jesus Christ, and to following where that leads, even into the unknown

- Engaged together, and with people of goodwill across the world, in acting, reflecting and praying for justice, peace and the integrity of creation

- Convinced that the inclusive community it seeks must be embodied in the community it practises

Together with its staff, the community is responsible for:

- The islands residential centres of Iona Abbey, the MacLeod Centre on Iona, and Camas Adventure Centre on the Ross of Mull

and in Glasgow:

- The administration of the Community

- Work with young people

- A publishing house, Wild Goose Publications

- Its association in the revitalising of worship with the Wild Goose Resource Group

The Iona Community was founded in Glasgow in 1938 by George MacLeod, minister, visionary and prophetic witness for peace, in the context of the poverty and despair of the Depression. Its original task of rebuilding the monastic ruins of Iona Abbey became a sign of hopeful rebuilding of community in Scotland and beyond. Today, it consists of about 280 Members, mostly in Britain, and 1500 Associate Members, with 1400 Friends worldwide. Together and apart, the community 'follows the light it has, and prays for more light'.

For information on the Iona Community contact:
The Iona Community, Fourth Floor, Savoy House,
140 Sauchiehall Street, Glasgow G2 3DH, UK.
Phone: 0141 332 6343
e-mail: admin@iona.org.uk; web: www.iona.org.uk

For enquiries about visiting Iona, please contact:
Iona Abbey, Isle of Iona, Argyll PA76 6SN, UK.
Phone: 01681 700404

For books, CDs & digital downloads published by Wild Goose Publications:
www.ionabooks.com